Enriching Forests, Empowering Communities:

Lessons from Participatory Forest Management in Kerala

George Alexander

Lijo P George

English, International Edition

Enriching Forests, Empowering Communities:

Lessons from Participatory Forest Management in Kerala

George Alexander & Lijo P George

First Edition – May 2024

Cover Photo - Glimpses of Participatory Forest Management Activities in Kerala

Cover Design - George Alexander

Publisher:

Old Monk Books, Cochin

Email: oldmonkbooks@gmail.com

ISBN - 978-1-304-35463-1

First published in Old Monk Paperback 2024

Published by

Cochin, Kerala

Email: oldmonkbooks@gmail.com

ISBN - 978-1-304-35463-1

Cover page – Glimpses of Participatory Forest Management Activities in Kerala.

Dedication

To the selfless stewards and people of the forests, both known and unknown, for their unwavering commitment, selfless contributions, sacrifices, and dedication to the cause of Participatory Forest Management (PFM), tirelessly working and sacrificing to make this vision a reality.

Disclaimer

This book represents the personal views and opinions of the authors and does not necessarily reflect the positions or opinions of any organization, institution, or individual with which the authors are affiliated. The content presented herein is based on the authors perspective and interpretation of the subject matter. Neither the publisher nor any associated parties shall be held responsible for any consequences arising from the opinions or interpretations expressed within this book.

The information provided within this book is for general informational, educational, and reading purposes only. The authors make no representations or warranties, express or implied, about the completeness, accuracy, reliability, suitability, or availability concerning the information, products, services, or related graphics contained in this book for any purpose. Any use of this information is at your own risk. This work may contain several images, data, and photographs that are used with the necessary permission from the owners, content from various sources, photographic content from the authors, and copyright-free images.

This work may also contain copyrighted materials, the use of which has not always been specifically authorized by the respective copyright owners. We have made use of such material to provide a better understanding of the best practices of Participatory Forest Management (PFM) and lessons from such activities in Kerala. If you wish to use copyrighted material from this work for your purposes, you must obtain permission from the respective copyright owners.

This book is also a collection of personal reflections, commentaries, outlooks, criticisms, and observations on PFM. The views expressed in this book are solely those of the authors and do not necessarily reflect the views of any governmental or non-governmental department, agency, organization, or individual. The authors have independently acquired all data and photographs used in this book from various sources including open sources, reports, books, web portals, documents, and interviews.

This book is not intended to serve as an official stance on PFM. Its purpose is to provide a range of perspectives on the topic and to encourage further discussion and debate. Instead, it aims to provide a multifaceted perspective on PFM. The authors recognize the complexity of PFM and the diversity of perspectives on its implementation and effectiveness. The authors make no claims to the accuracy or completeness of the information contained in this book. Readers are encouraged to conduct their research to form their own opinions on PFM.

The authors disclaim all liability for any damages or losses that may arise from the use of the information contained in this book. Any decisions made based on the information contained in this book should be made with the advice of qualified professionals and experts.

The criticisms presented in this book are not directed at any government mechanism, government department, government servants, or bureaucracy. Rather, it aims to highlight potential areas for improvement and foster constructive dialogue on enhancing the governance of PFM. The author's intention is not to disparage or undermine any organization but rather to contribute to the betterment of governance and public administration.

Although the publisher and the authors have made every effort to ensure that the information in this book was correct at press time and while this publication is designed to provide accurate information regarding the subject matter covered, the publisher and the author assume no responsibility for errors, inaccuracies, omissions, or any other inconsistencies herein and hereby disclaim any liability to any party for any loss, damage, or disruption caused by errors or omissions, whether such errors or omissions result from negligence, accident, or any other cause.

Contents

Foreword

"Enriching Forests, Empowering Communities: Lessons from Participatory Forest Management (PFM) in Kerala," the book authored by George Alexander and Lijo P George is a collection of inspiring narratives on community-centered forest management in Kerala. It presents not only a collection of best practices in participatory forest management but also the saga of positive transformation brought about by participatory endeavors for the environment and communities.

PFM in Kerala, born in the mid-1990s, travelled a long route starting from recognizing the inherent rights and potential of local, indigenous communities, the natural caretakers of forests. PFM initiated a new approach, where communities became active participants, not passive beneficiaries, in forest conservation and management.

The book comes out at a time when there is a felt need for more sustainable forest management practices than ever before. Deforestation, climate change, and the loss of biodiversity endanger our ecology and demand innovative solutions with a fine balance between protecting the environment and meeting the needs of local communities.

Kerala is a pioneer in Participatory Forest Management (PFM), a model that empowers the local communities to have a stake in the decision-making for managing their surrounding forests. The book presents the lessons from Kerala's PFM journey, offering valuable insights and examples for both academia and practitioners.

Elucidating with interesting case studies, the book showcases projects that have brought about a transformation in the lives of forest-dependent communities. Ranging from ecotourism ventures that empower the excluded local communities to sustainable harvesting of Non-Timber Forest Products (NTFPs) that ensure ecological balance, each project is a testament to the ingenuity and dedication of communities gaining rights over natural resources.

Readers can hear the voices of the communities and of a bunch of dedicated forest officials who were instrumental in this transformation. The narratives reveal the challenges overcome, the victories celebrated, and the enduring spirit of collaboration that underpins the PFM model of Kerala.

Nevertheless, the book doesn't shy away from making a critical appraisal of Participatory Forest Management. It impartially examines the loopholes and impediments in the execution of PFM practices that offer valuable inputs for their improvement. Besides being a collection of success stories, the book sets the agenda for serious discussions on the topic. It also invites all the stakeholders including policymakers, officials, researchers, and most importantly, the community concerned to engage in progressive dialogues, share experiences, and move towards sustainable forests and communities.

More than a technical manual, "Enriching Forests, Empowering Communities" is the evidence of transformation brought about by participatory engagements. This book demonstrates that when communities are empowered to manage natural resources, they become not only the caretakers of the environment but also the architects of sustainable development.

Dr. M S Jayakumar

Assistant Professor, Department of Sociology
& Director, Centre for Diaspora Studies
University of Kerala, Kariavattom Campus
Thiruvananthapuram, Kerala

Preface and Introduction

Participatory Forest Management (PFM) is an approach to forest management that involves tribal, indigenous, traditional, and other local forest-dependent communities in the decision-making and implementation of forest conservation and management activities (Schreckenberg & Luttrell, 2009). PFM is based on the principle that forest-dependent communities have the right to participate in the management and conservation of forests (Saxena, 1997).

In the mid-1990s, the Kerala Forest & Wildlife Department (KFD) launched the PFM program in the state. PFM is a community-based approach to forest management that involves local communities in the planning, implementation, monitoring, and sustainable conservation of forest resources (George & Alexander, 2023). This approach has been successful in Kerala, and it has helped to improve the relationship between the KFD and local communities to a larger extent.

Over the last twenty-five years, despite various challenges, PFM has aided in increasing forest cover in the state, reducing the incidence of forest fires, protecting wildlife populations, and creating employment opportunities for local forest-dependent communities thereby improving their social and economic conditions(ibid). PFM promotes democratic management since it guarantees intense community participation at all levels of operation. Despite the challenges, PFM in Kerala remains a successful example of how community-based management can be used to achieve sustainable forest management.

This short book tries to present a brief, but comprehensive overview of the best practices and lessons from PFM in Kerala. It focuses on specific projects that have had a positive impact on the lives of forest-dependent communities. Nevertheless, it examines a range of PFM projects in Kerala, including ecotourism, Non-timber Forest Products (NTFP) management, tribal empowerment, alternative income generation, and sustainable practices. The report concludes with a discussion of the key factors that have contributed to the success of PFM in Kerala. The book also extends beyond a mere overview of best practices of PFM to delve into a critical examination of the challenges, and execution-related hurdles that arise in participatory management. This book does not claim to be an authoritative study on the best practices in PFM in Kerala, nor does it provide an in-depth critical evaluation of PFM practices in the state. Instead, it serves as reading material to help readers understand the projects and programs that have positively impacted the lives of forest-dependent communities. At the same time, it strives to present an objective view of PFM. Nevertheless, we have tried our best to provide valuable case studies of how PFM can be used to achieve positive outcomes for both forests and communities. This book would be interesting for anyone interested in participatory management, sustainable forest conservation, and the lives of forest-dependent communities. This book also aims to generate interest from researchers, academicians, and above all the public on PFM and invites their careful attention to the matter. Apart from the best PFM practices, this book delves into the projects and programs executed by the Forest Department[1] for the welfare of forest-dependent communities. The book also discusses topics, such as NTFP management, ecotourism, Forest Rights Act (FRA), etc.

Due to the time constraints of completing this book in just two months, it was not possible to include all best practices. Therefore, we have carefully selected and prioritized projects and programs that play a significant role in reshaping PFM in the State.

---

[1] For the sake of clarity within this book, "Forest Department" will always refer to the Kerala Forest & Wildlife Department. You may also encounter it referred to in full as the Kerala Forest Department or Kerala Forest and Wildlife Department, but these all denote the same entity.

We are deeply indebted to the unwavering support of those who made this book a reality. Their dedication and encouragement were instrumental in its creation:

Shri. Pramod G Krishnan IFS, Shri. P. N. Unnikrishnan IFS, Shri. Jayaprasad IFS, Shri. S R Radhakrishnan (Deputy Conservator of Forests), Shri. Baiju Krishnan (Assistant Conservator of Forests), Shri. Jacob Mathew (Sociologist and PFM Specialist), Shri. Viju Varghese (Deputy Conservator of Forests), Shri. Dileepkumar KG (Deputy Range Forest Officer, Thenmala & Asst. PFM Coordinator, Southern Circle), Shri. Ajin V C (Asst. PFM Manager –Marketing & Branding, SFDA), Shri. Ravikumar (Deputy Range Forest Officer, Silent Valley), Smt. Praseeda E P (Beat Forest Officer & PFM Coordinator, Chalakudy), Shri Kanakaraj (Beat Forest Officer & PFM Coordinator, Punalur), Shri. Jaydevan (Beat Forest Officer & PFM Coordinator, Peechi), Shri. Habbas (Section Forest Officer & PFM Coordinator, Mannarkad), Shri. Rajeev (Beat Forest Officer & PFM Coordinator, Vazhachal), Shri.Unnikirshna Pillai (Section Forest Officer & PFM Coordinator, Nilmbur North), Shri. Sinukumar (Section Forest Officer, Peppara), Shri. Sanal Kumar (Beat Forest Officer & PFM Coordinator, North Wayanad), Shri. Kiran K P (Regional Director, Forest-PLUS 2.0., Kerala), Shri. Vinod (Beat Forest Officer & PFM Coordinator, Konni), and Smt. Lekshmi (Head Accountant, E & TW, Forest Headquarters).

George Alexander
&
Lijo P George
May 2024

The Kerala Forest & Wildlife Department (KFD)

The Kerala Forest Department (KFD) is one of the oldest government departments in Kerala. It is responsible for the sustainable management of forests, biodiversity, and wildlife in the state (Chundamannil, 1983). The KFD works closely with the indigenous tribal and other forest-dependent communities to achieve its goals (George & Alexander, 2023).

Operational Structure of the Kerala Forest Department

The Kerala Forest Department (KFD) is organized into territorial, wildlife, and social forestry circles and divisions at the operational and execution levels. There are eight circles, of which five are territorial and three are wildlife. Within the eight circles, there are 25 territorial divisions and 11 wildlife divisions. An equal number of Forest Development Agencies are constituted within 36 Divisions of KFD for the execution of the PFM program.

Social Forestry is organized into three circles with 14 divisions. An equal number of Social Forestry Forest Development Agencies (SFFDAs) are constituted for the execution of social forestry programs as well. In social forestry, the grass-root level institutions are known as Participatory Haritha Samithis (PHS) whereas in PFM they are called Vana Samrakshana Samithis (VSS) and Eco-development Committees (EDC). The Social Forestry Wing of the Kerala Forest Department (KFD) supports afforestation and tree planting in non-forest areas. It is the lead agency for all people-centered schemes implemented outside protected areas. The Social Forestry Wing is also responsible for implementing all government-approved plans and non-plan schemes in non-forest areas, and it monitors and reviews the progress of these schemes.

Circles, Divisions, & Forest Development Agencies

Forest Circles (Territorial & Wildlife)	Forest Divisions (Territorial & Wildlife)	Forest Development Agencies (FDAs)	Social Forestry Regions (Circles)	Social Forestry Divisions	Social Forestry Forest Development Agencies (SFFDAs)
8	36	36	3	14	14

The Evolution of Participatory Forest Management in India

Forest-Dependent Communities (FDC)

Before analyzing Participatory/Joint Forest Management, it is important to learn about forest-dependent communities. They are people who live near or in forests and rely on them for their livelihoods. They are often indigenous people (tribal communities), shifting cultivators, nomadic forest-dwelling people, hunters and gatherers, rural small farmers, and rural people living in or at the margins of forests. While most forest-dependent communities in Kerala are tribal, there are also non-tribal communities that depend on the forest for their livelihood (Shylajan & Mythili, 2007)(MoEF, 2010).

JFM, and Forest-Dependent Communities

The participatory approach to forest management at the grassroots level in India was initiated in the 1970s (Sharma, 1995: Dhanapal, 2019). Joint Forest Management (JFM) is the term used in India for community partnerships in forest conservation. The history of Joint Forest Management (JFM) in India can be traced back to 1972, with the formation of several informal forest protection committees (FPCs) in West Bengal. FPCs were set up by local communities under the leadership of Dr. Ajit Kumar Banerjee, in response to the degradation of forests due to illegal logging, grazing, and other human activities. Hence, Dr. Banerjee is credited as the father of Joint Forest Management (JFM) in India (Guha *et al.*, 2000). Dr. Banerjee, while serving as a Divisional Forest Officer in West Bengal, faced constant challenges from grazing and illegal harvesting by the local communities. As a result, to overcome the situation and to share forest resources, he sought out representatives of eleven villages and negotiated a contract with an ad hoc Forest Protection Committee through the Arabari project. In return for helping in forest protection by villagers, they were employed in both silvicultural and harvesting operations of the forest. They received 25 percent of the final product and were allowed to collect firewood and fodder from the forest area on a nominal payment (Bisui *et al.*,2023). With the active and willing participation of local people living around the forest, the degraded sal forest of Arabari transformed into a thick and green forest within a decade. The government initially rejected the JFM scheme, but international acclaim prompted its acceptance and expansion to other parts of the state from 1987 onwards.

In 1988, the Government of India issued a circular outlining the principles of JFM. The circular emphasized the need for mutual trust and cooperation between Forest Departments in India and local communities and the equitable sharing of benefits from forest resources. Over the next few years, JFM spread to other states in India, and by the early 1990s, it was being implemented on a large scale. In 1998, the Government of India issued revised guidelines for JFM, which further strengthened the role of local communities in sustainable forest management. Hence, it may be stated that JFM is a collaborative forest management approach between the government and local communities, through which the government aims to restore degraded forests and provide a better livelihood to forest-dependent communities (Bhattacharya *et al.*2010). The policies and objectives of JFM are outlined in the National Forest Policy of 1988 and the Joint Forest Management Guidelines of 1990. Over 25 million families are involved in JFM committees across the country, and over 27 million hectares of forest land are under joint management.

PFM - The Kerala Scenario

In Kerala, JFM is known as Participatory Forest Management (PFM). It was introduced in Kerala in 1998 in line with the National Forest Policy of 1988. PFM is a democratic and decentralized approach to forest management that involves local communities in the sustainable development, protection, and management of forests. (Alexander, 2021).

PFM is a two-way approach. The Forest Department works with local communities to develop and implement forest management plans, programs, and projects that meet the needs of both parties. In return, local communities agree to protect the forests and use them sustainably. Hence, PFM is not just about forest protection. It also aims to improve the socio-economic conditions of local communities, especially tribal communities. This includes providing alternative sources of income, reducing forest dependency, and empowering women. Commitment to forest-dependent communities, social causes, sustainable conservation of forests, upliftment of tribal communities, creating alternative sources of income, reducing forest dependency, and empowerment of women are some of the key guiding principles of PFM. (Alexander, 2021).

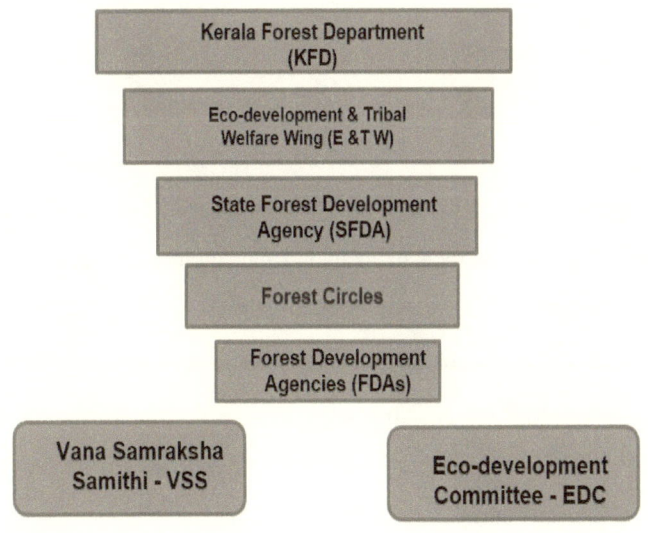

PFM – A Democratic and Decentralized Approach

India is a sovereign, socialist, secular, democratic republic with a parliamentary form of government that is federal in structure with unitary features. The country follows a three-tier system of administration comprising the central government, state government, panchayat raj, and municipalities. In line with the democratic values and decentralized administrative system in the country, the Forest Department executes PFM through a six-tier system which ensures a decentralized and democratic process of managing forest resources.

PFM – Operational Structure

Examining the operational structure of PFM, we can see that the Kerala Forest Department is its custodian in the state. The Eco-development and Tribal Welfare Wing is responsible for formulating policies and overall supervision of PFM. The State Forest Development Agency (SFDA), an autonomous body constituted in 2010, is the apex body of 36 Forest Development Agencies (FDAs) in the state. It is also the nodal agency for various projects and oversees the execution of PFM programs. In the words of Pramod G Krishnan IFS, the State Forest Development Agency (SFDA) serves as a "special purpose vehicle" dedicated to advancing Participatory Forest Management (PFM) initiatives. The Principal Chief Conservator of Forests & Head of Forest Force (HoFF) is chosen as the Chairman and the Additional Principal Chief Conservator of Forests (E&TW) is chosen as the Member Secretary of SFDA. The general body of the SFDA consists of the Principal Secretary of Forest, all Principal and Additional Conservators of forests, Chief Conservators of Forests, all Divisional Forest Officers, Wildlife Wardens, and representatives from over 12 government line departments. This is to ensure utmost transparency in its operation.

An FDA is a confederation of PFM institutions (Vana Samrakshana Samithi - VSS) and Eco-Development Committee - EDC) affiliated with the SFDA, through which PFM activities are implemented at the grassroots level. They are autonomous bodies constituted in line with the Forest Divisions for the execution of PFM Programs. VSS/EDC are the democratic grassroots-level PFM institutions that ensure the participation of tribal and forest-dependent communities. The Chief Conservator of Forests (CCF) of each Circle is chosen as the Chairman of the FDA, whereas the DFO/Wildlife Warden is chosen as the CEO (Chief Executive Officer). The General Body of the FDA consists of a President, a Secretary, and a Female Member from each VSS/EDC (PFM Institutions) under the FDA, whereas Assistant Range Officers, Range Officers, and 15 District-Level Officers are selected as Ex-Officio members.

Models of PFM

In Kerala there exist three basic models of PFM institutions, namely Vana Samraksha Samithi (VSS) in fringe areas (forest land outside wildlife areas) comprising tribal and non-tribal communities, Adivasi Vana Samraksha Samithi (AVSS), comprising only tribal members and Eco-development Committee (EDC), constituted in wildlife area comprising tribal and non-tribal communities (Soman & Anitha, 2020). All PFM institutions are affiliated with the FDA. The FDA issues a registration number and certificate. Forest-dependent communities are organized into these three models of PFM depending on the community, locality, and various other factors. In fringe areas, two members from each family are given membership in the general body of VSS/EDC, whereas for tribal communities all members in a family above the age of 18 are eligible to become members. The Executive Committee of VSS/EDC consists of nine members, three of whom must be women, including a panchayat ward member, a representative of the SC/ST department, a president, a treasurer, and a member secretary (Forest Officer). The committee is elected for a period of two years. Forest-dependent communities are deeply involved in every stage, right from the formation of VSS/EDC, preparation of microplan, annual plan of operation, and the management of day-to-day affairs. Moreover, elected representatives (ward members) are an integral part of the Executive Committee of every PFM institution as well (Gurukkal, 2003).

Management of PFM in the State – Institutional Arrangement

The Forest Department through SFDA has established a robust organizational structure to oversee and promote PFM activities. To spearhead these efforts a State PFM Cell has been constituted, comprising an Assistant Conservator of Forests (ACF) designated as the State PFM Coordinator, a PFM Manager, and two Assistant PFM Managers. This team is tasked with overseeing the implementation and coordination of PFM initiatives across the state. It shall be noted that the Government Order (MS) No. 9/2009/F&WLD, dated 3.02.2009, mandates the establishment of a PFM Cell.

Furthermore, Circle-level, Division-level, and Range-level PFM Coordinators, Asst. Coordinators have been appointed to foster collaboration and ensure seamless implementation of PFM activities within their respective jurisdictions. Some FDAs have also appointed Sociologists at the Division level to strengthen and professionalize PFM activities. They play a crucial role in bridging the gap between the state-level PFM Cell and the on-ground implementation teams.

To address the critical need for training and capacity building, SFDA has established a State-level PFM Expert Committee. This committee comprises seasoned experts and practitioners who provide valuable guidance and support in designing and delivering training programs for forest officials, community members, and other stakeholders involved in PFM initiatives.

Documentation

One of the most important aspects of PFM is that every process is well-documented. The Forest Department has various well-defined guidelines that outline the implementation of PFM projects.

PFM institutions function based on microplans created and renewed every five years. The preperation of microplans involves the participation of forest-dependent communities at every step. Participatory Rural Appraisal (PRA) is the approach used to create microplans, which are based on local knowledge and forest resources. In addition to microplans, PFM institutions also create annual plans of operation for smooth functioning. Every decision taken in FDAs or PFM institutions by Executive Committees or General Bodies is well-documented. These are open, democratic platforms that foster the participation of forest-dependent communities in decision-making.

Stakeholders of PFM

PFM is composed of various stakeholders. The major stakeholders are listed below:

The State: The State is the apex body that is the prime stakeholder. It ensures the governance required for the smooth conduct of PFM.

The Kerala Forest Department & Allied Organizations: The Forest Department is one of the primary stakeholders in PFM as they are bound with the sustainable conservation of forests. They formulate policies and provide professional, administrative, and technical support and guidance to PFM institutions through the Eco-development & Tribal Welfare Wing, State Forest Development Agency (SFDA), and Forest Development Agencies (FDA) for the planning, execution, monitoring, and evaluation of various projects and programs.

Forest-dependent Communities (Members of PFM Institutions): PFM institutions (VSS/EDC) are composed of the forest-dependent community, as well as local self-government and forest officials. They play a key role in planning and implementing forest management activities, such as afforestation, protection, and sustainable harvesting of non-timber forest products.

Local Self-Government and People's Representatives: The local government bodies play a role in supporting PFM by providing funds, resources, and assistance. Panchayat Raj Institution (PRI) members also represent the local community in PFM institutions.

SHG Members: SHGs (Self-Help Groups) are women's or men's groups that are involved in a variety of activities, including forest management. SHGs are constituted as part of the PFM institutions. Under the patronage of the respective VSS/EDC, they engage in various income generation and welfare activities.

Research/Academic Institutions/NGOs (Non-Governmental Organizations): They play a role in PFM by providing technical support, training, and other resources to PFM institutions. In partnership with the Forest Department, they organize various programs on sustainable forest management practices and welfare of the forest-dependent communities.

Private and Public Sector Organizations: Private and Public sector organizations provide financial and logistic support to PFM institutions through CSR funds for various welfare programs. They also provide technical assistance and engage in partnership with PFM institutions, FDAs, or SFDA.

The Public: The public is a beneficiary as they contribute to the function of PFM by paying taxes. They also get to enjoy unadulterated non-timber forest produce, ecotourism, timber, and other forest resources.

A Comprehensive Approach

It is important to understand that PFM is a comprehensive approach that encompasses not just sustainable forest conservation, infrastructure development, and alternative income generation but also the overall social development of forest-dependent communities. Sustainable forest management cannot be achieved without addressing the social needs of these communities, such as education, skill development, healthcare, cultural preservation, entrepreneurship development, gender equality, empowerment, self-determination, awareness generation, avenues for participation, decision-making capacity, conflict resolution, self-reliance, etc. PFM provides a decentralized democratic platform for forest-dependent communities to meet their social, financial, and psychological needs by fostering public-private partnerships.

The Status of PFM in Kerala

PFM Institutions (VSS/EDC Count)

At present, there are 640 VSS/EDC in the state.

Total Number of VSS /EDC (Forest Circle Wise)

Forest Circle	VSS/EDC
Southern	112
High Range	71
Central	64
Eastern	93
North	87
Wildlife Palakkad	48
ABP Wildlife	43
Filed Director	122
Total	640

Source: (George & Alexander, 2023)

There are a total of 640 VSS/EDC statewide out of which 427 are VSS and 213 are EDC.

Families Engaged in PFM Institutions

Type	Number	Percentage
Scheduled Caste	10,524	14.71 %
Scheduled Tribe	19,093	26.70 %
Other	41,886	58.57 %
Total	71,503	

Source: (George & Alexander, 2023)

There are 10,524 (14.7 percent) Scheduled Caste, 19,093 (26.70 percent) Scheduled Tribe, and 41,886 (58.7 percent) other families that depend upon VSS/EDC in the state.

Forest Area Managed by PFM Institutions (VSS/EDC)

A considerable area of the forest area in Kerala is managed by PFM institutions. They cater to 20.14 percent of Kerala's forest area.

VSS/EDC Activities

According to the collected data, 34.37 percent of the VSS/EDC are engaged in fire protection works that include engaging fire gangs, creating, and maintenance of fire lines, controlled burning, and fire awareness campaigns. 33.43 percent of the VSS/EDC are engaged in social and charitable activities like infrastructure developments, training, and awareness programs, waste removal activities, providing financial support for the needy, farming, etc. 10percent of the VSS/EDC engage both in fire-based and community-oriented activities.

Kerala Forest Ecotourism

There are 71 eco-tourism centers in the state which are operated and managed by the members of the VSS/EDC with guidance and support from FDAs.

SL No	Item	Unit
1.	Ecotourism Centers	71
2.	Number of Ecotourism Packages	215
3.	VSS/EDC Members Engaged	2172
4.	FDAs Involved	33

5.	VSS/EDC involved	93
6.	Types of Packages Offered (14 types)	Trekking, Stay, Site Seeing, Safari, Boating, Waterfall, Camping, Nature Park, Cycling, Hiking, Bird Watching, Botanical Garden, Watch Tower, Butterfly Garden.

Source: (Alexander, 2022)

Vanasree

There are 74 Vanasree Units in the state out of which two are mobile units (Trivandrum and Malayatoor). The forest-dependent communities are provided with ample opportunity to market and sell their NTFPs by overcoming the middlemen and other exploiters. Profit generated from sales of NTFPs through Vanasree units is plowed back to collectors (forest-dependent communities) (Ajin, 2020).

SL No	Item	Unit
1.	Total Vanasree Outlets	74 Vanasree Eco shops Out of which 2 are Mobile Vanasree outlets
2.	Total tribal population Involved in NTFP Collection	More than 50,000 NTFP Collectors
3.	Number of NTFP Collected	Over 56 varieties of NTFPs

Source: (Primary Data).

Major Projects and Programs Implemented through PFM for the tribal and forest-depended communities:

- Non-timber Forest Products (NTFP) Management & Vanasree Outlets.

- TRIFED Projects (VDVK & MSP for MFP) – Van Dhan Vikas Kendra (VDVK), Minimum Support Price for Minor Forest Produce are two projects of the Tribal Cooperative Marketing Development Federation of India (TRIFED).

- Forest Conservation and Forestry Works – They include fire protection activities, gully pulling, check dam construction, fire line, fire gang, etc.

- Green India Mission (GIM) - It is a flagship program of the Government of India under the National Action Plan on Climate Change (NAPCC) which aims to increase forest cover, ecological restoration, enhance tree cover, restore wetlands, promote alternative fuel energy etc.

- Ecotourism – Providing an alternative source of income to indigenous tribal and other forest-dependent communities to reduce their dependency on forest resources.

- Nagaravan Yojana - A government-sponsored scheme that aims to promote urban forestry in India. The scheme was launched in 2020 and is being implemented by the Ministry of Environment, Forest, and Climate Change. It provides financial assistance to municipal corporations, municipalities, and other local bodies to develop urban forests.

- Vana Oushdha Samrithi – This project aims to promote the cultivation and sale of medicinal plants, with a particular focus on turmeric and holy basil (tulsi). This initiative seeks to empower local forest-dependent communities and provide them with a sustainable livelihood while also preserving the biodiversity of medicinal herbs.

31

- Outreach Activities - Social, economic, and charitable activities - waste management, income generation projects, distribution of food kits, health camps, sports events, soft skill development, coaching for competitive examinations, building libraries and reading rooms, initiating space for local markets, intervention programs, etc.

Behind the Curtain – The Unsung Heroes of PFM

The success of Participatory Forest Management (PFM) in Kerala can be attributed to the tireless efforts of a pioneering group of PFM specialists and forest officers. These individuals have played a pivotal role in laying the groundwork for PFM's implementation, monitoring, and evaluation. Their dedication and expertise were instrumental in crafting operational guidelines, supporting FDAs in establishing PFM institutions, organizing training programs, guiding PRA exercises and micro-plan creation, and providing essential consultations and resources. Their unwavering commitment laid the solid foundation upon which PFM in Kerala has thrived.

Officials Instrumental in Implementing the PFM Program in Kerala

Name	Designation
Sasidharan IFS	PCCF (Gen)
P K Surendranathan Asari IFS	PCCF (Dev)
Balchandhran Thampi IFS	CCF (World Bank)
P N Unnikrishnan IFS (Prepared necessary GOs and guidelines for implementation and provided adequate training)	CCF (E&TW, PFM State Coordinator)
K P Ouseph IFS	CCF (E&TW, PFM State Coordinator)
Jacob Mathew (Prepared necessary GOs and guidelines for implementation and provided adequate training)	PFM Specialist
Sundaresan Nair	NAP Facilitator

R R Sukla IFS	C F
K J Varghese IFS	
Subranian IFS	
S Murali	ACF (Circle Coordinator)
James Zacharia	ACF (Circle Coordinator)
K G Dileep Kumar	BFO
Gopinatha Pillai	
Suresh Babu	
Hari Kumar IFS	C F
Lakhvindar Singh IFS	
M S Jayaraman	ACF (Circle Coordinator)
Joshy Sebastian	SFO
Anil S	BFO
Binoylal	
Harikumaran Nair	
Nazir Shah	
P R Jayaprakash	
Somi	
A K Goyal IFS	CF
Nagesh Prabhu IFS	
B P Davis	ACF (Circle Coordinator)
S Syam	
Sheik Hyder Hussian	D FO Vazachal
P O Appachan	SFO
K Raju	BFO
M P Anil Kumar	

Rajendhrababu	
Satheeshkumar	
P Vinod	
Sanil IP	SFO
K T Pious	
T P Venugopal	
Gopinathan IFS	CF
Alikhan	ACF (Circle Coordinator)
Sreevalsan	
T S Xavier	SFO
Anil Kumar	
Mohanakrishnan	BFO
Manojkumar K	
Vasudevan	
Bhadrakumar	
S Rajendran	
K Vijayakumar	
Teggi IFS	C F
P K Kesavan IFS	C F
K Krishnakumar	ACF (Circle Coordinator)
Saji Rayaroth	SFO
Sreejith	BFO
Unnikrishnan	
M G Vinodkumar	
Jayaprakash	
Beerankutty	

Salim	
Jimmy Abraham	President, Elappedika VSS
Unni Krishnan	Computer Operator (E & TW Wing)

Officers involved in the India Eco-Development Project at the Periyar Tiger Reserve (PTR)

Name	Designation at that time
Bennichan Thomas IFS	W.L.P.O Thekady , EDO Thekady and FD(PT) Kottayam
E.P Kumaran, ACF	AFD Thekady and DD West
Simon Francis,RO	Range Officer Vallakkadavu
O P Kaler IFS	W.L.P.O Thekady, FD(PT) Kottayam
A.K Bharadwaj IFS	W.L.P.O Thekady, FD(PT) Kottayam
V K Uniyal IFS	FD(PT) Kottayam
Harikumar IFS	FD(PT) Kottayam
Pramod G Krishnan IFS	EDO Thekady, WLPO Thekady
James Zacharia (ACF)	Range Officer, Research
John Nirmal Agustin	Thekkady Range Officer
S Sivadas IFS	AFD Thekkady
S Sreekumar	Range Officer Vallakkadavu
K K Sabu SFO (ACF)	Moozhikal Forester
Joseph Vargheese FG (SFO)	Moozhikal Section EDC Secretary
Y Babu FG (SFO)	EDC Secretary
Paul P Isac FG (SFO)	EDC Secretary
A V Somy FG (SFO)	EDC Secretary
U M jithendranadh FG (SFO)	EDC Secretary

S Guruvayoorappan	Sociologist
Balasubramanian	Conservation Biologist
K L Syamala	NGI (MIST Team)
Anilkumar M B	NGI (MIST Team)
Thankachan V O	NGI (MIST Team)
P N Vijayan	NGI (MIST Team)
Jaya Rajappan	NGI (MIST Team)
K V Sebastian	NGI (MIST Team)
Sidhardhan SFO	EDC Secretary
Sisupalan	Junior Superindent

Special Mention

Dileep Kumar K.G. (Deputy Range Officer of the Thenmala Forest Division and Assistant PFM Coordinator of the Southern Circle) deserves special mention. He joined the Kerala Forest Department in 1997 and was inspired by the PFM training provided by Shri P N Unnikrishnan IFS in 1999 at the State Forest Training Institute, Arippa. For the past 25 years, he has been fully engaged in various PFM activities. He has played a prominent role in developing the administrative and technical aspects of Participatory Forest Management (PFM), particularly by framing policies, providing training for forest officers in PFM, and enhancing Participatory Rural Appraisal (PRA) to suit the needs of the forest department in preparing microplans for PFM institutions. He stands out as a key trainer actively contributing to forest management capacity building. He is involved in developing training modules and lesson plans for Participatory Forest Management (PFM) for officers, while also serving as a guest faculty on PFM at forest training institutes. His expertise is sought after by various forest divisions for training on PFM and related subjects. Furthermore, he played a leading role in establishing PRA core teams across all forest divisions and provided them with essential training. His dedication extends to the Green India Mission, where he assisted with training divisional staff for its implementation. Dileep Kumar has taken a leading role in implementing the Forest Rights Act (FRA), particularly regarding community rights and community forest resources. Additionally, he prepared a format for crafting Community Forest Resource Management Plans under the FRA framework. One of his recent achievements was the national coverage on the front page (03/01/2023) of the Hindu Daily for the IIST Science Workshop under his leadership which was held in the Villumala Tribal hamlet under the Thenmala Division. A leading expert on PFM in the Forest Department, Dileep Kumar was decorated with the Chief Minister's Forest Medal for exemplary service in 2005 and 2018.

Chapter -1

The Tribal Women Initiatives of Chalakudy

Chalakudy

Chalakudy (*Shalakudi*) is a municipal town, located in the Thrissur district in Kerala. The word Chalakudy is derived from two words namely *Yagasala* and *Kodi*. It is situated on the banks of the Chalakudy River (Chalakudy Puzha) which is the 5th longest river in the State. It is also one of the pristine rivers in the state which is well known for its diversity, as it contains over 98 species of freshwater fish (Census, 2011). The two world-famous waterfalls Vazhachal and Athirappilly lie within the Chalakudy River. The Chalakudy Forest Division, one among the 36 Forest Divisions of the Kerala Forest Department was established in 1950, three years after the Indian independence. The Chalakudy Forest Division is constituted of the Pariyaram, Palapilly, and Vellikulnangara forest ranges'. The Chalakudy FDA was established in 2002 to cater to and manage PFM activities. Malayan and Kadar are the two forest-dependent tribal communities found in Chalakudy. Both of them are primitive tribal groups who are traditionally exorcists, spirit dancers, and mendicants. There are 11 settlements (colonies) of Kadar and Malayan tribal communities organized into 13 VSS that fall under the jurisdiction of the Chalakudy Forest Division.

Non-timber Forest Produce (NTFP) Collection and Management in Chalakudy FDA

The Chalakudy FDA is engaged in the sustainable collection, value-addition, and management of NTFPs also known as Minor Forest Produce (MFP) collected by various tribal communities as well as its sales under Vanasree (the official NTFP brand of the Kerala Forest Department). The major NTFPs collected are honey, turmeric, dammer, soap pod, wild nutmeg, acacia wild, etc. The government provides a

39

minimum support price (MSP for MFP scheme) for the NTFPs collected to avoid exploitation by the middlemen. The profit generated from the sales of NTFP is reverted to the tribal communities. Moreover, they are also given bonus payments (financial rewards) throughout the time of the festive seasons, especially during Onam (the annual harvest festival in Kerala). It is one of the few Forest Divisions that provides bonus payments to tribal communities during festival seasons (George & Alexander, 2023).

Chalakudy FDA, in addition, is the pioneer in establishing an e-commerce sales platform (vanasree.in) for Vanasree products, thereby extending its reach to a more considerable section of the population in Kerala. The Vanasree unit of the Chalakudy FDA also takes part in several local and national exhibitions throughout the year as well. Between 2019 and 2023, the Chalakudy FDA generated Rs 18,881,549 ($2,27,883.30) through the sales of NTFPs under the Vanasree brand.

The GST-Lucky Bill Project

Yet another initiative is a tribal women-driven gift hamper packing unit for the winners of the Lucky Bill Mobile App project of the Directorate General of Goods and Service Tax (DGST) in the state. The "Lucky Bill App" launched by the Kerala government in August 2022 encourages people to request bills for their purchases and help curb GST evasion. Users can upload their bills to the app to enter a lottery for prizes, including cash and gift packs. One of the gift hampers is provided by the Kerala Forest Department's Vanasree initiative. The Vanasree gift hamper consists of NTFPs collected, value-added, and packed by the Kadar tribal women of the Anapantham hamlet in Chalakudy. The project is fully women-run, with the women of the Anapantham hamlet responsible for collecting and processing NTFPs, packing gift hampers, and delivering them to winners across the state. Since 2022, the project has generated ₹77,20,000 in revenue for the Chalakudy FDA, and it has also provided over

1,200 work days for the women of the Anapantham tribal hamlet. India Post delivers gift hampers to the public, making it more convenient to reach even the most remote corners of the state. Moreover, the Vanasree gift hampers have been well received by the public, with many people praising the quality of the products and the packaging.

Impact of the Project on Tribal Women

The project has had several positive impacts on the tribal communities of Anapantham. It has provided tribal communities with a sustainable source of income from the NTFPs. The project has also helped to raise awareness of the importance of PFM and the role that tribal communities can play in forest management. This venture is a first-of-its-kind public-sector consortium project between the GST Department, the Kerala Forest Department, and India Post. It is also one of the most successful projects of its kind in the state. The GST Luck Bill APP-Vanasree Mutual Venture is a classic example of how PFM can be used to empower tribal communities and improve their livelihoods. The project has shown that women can play a leading role in PFM, and it has also shown that NTFPs can be a valuable source of income for tribal communities.

The gift hamper project has had a profound impact on the tribal women of Anapanatham hamlet, not only providing them with additional income but also instilling a high level of confidence. This newfound confidence has empowered them to aspire to take on more challenging projects in the future. The project has played a significant role in developing their entrepreneurial skills, fostering trust, fellowship, teamwork, and enhancing their overall skills. The project has provided them with a platform to showcase their craftsmanship and entrepreneurial spirit, enabling them to create gift hampers. The positive feedback they have received from customers has boosted their self-esteem and instilled a sense of pride in their work.

Other Tribal Women-Driven Initiatives

The FDA is also engaged in the sales of indigenous food products prepared by tribal women. The tribal women in Chalakudy spearhead several small-scale industry units. Presently they are engaged in embroidery, bamboo craft, pickle production, cosmetic, and coffee powder processing. Items manufactured in these units are distributed through the Vanasree shop and the online e-commerce platform. Such opportunities aid tribal women to have additional earnings leading to financial independence. Chalakudy FDA is a shining example of success in the Kerala Forest Department. Led by Praseetha EP (BFO & Division PFM Coordinator) and supported by forest authorities and tribal communities, Chalakudy has set the bar high for the collection, processing, marketing, and sales of NTFPs in Kerala. It has become a role model for other forest divisions for years to come.

The Unsung Heroine of Chalakudy

One of the key reasons for the success of the Chalakudy FDA is the leadership provided by **Smt. Praseetha E P.** She plays a pivotal role in coordinating the PFM activities, particularly NTFP management within the division. However, her efforts extend beyond mere NTFP management. Praseetha demonstrates unwavering dedication to the overall welfare of the region's tribal communities. Her active engagement with these communities, especially with tribal women, has resulted in a remarkable shift. The Kadar women of Anapaantham VSS, one of the most primitive tribal communities, are now actively participating in entrepreneurship and income-generating activities. Praseetha's initiative has motivated these women to step outside their traditional roles and engage with mainstream society. This has empowered them to become regular income earners for their families, significantly improving their lives. Interestingly, the highly successful GST lucky bill app gift hamper project was built upon an existing production model previously developed by an NGO. By the time the tribal women became involved in this project, the NGO moved out. Praseetha, however, recognized the potential of the existing structure and utilized it to create one of the most successful income-generating projects in the recent history of the Kerala Forest Department.

Beyond her official duties, she has become a champion for the Chalakudy division's tribal communities, playing a vital role in boosting their NTFP sales. Through ongoing training and encouragement, she has empowered them to improve their NTFP management and processing skills. Deeper than policy, her leadership has touched the hearts of forest-dependent communities. By stepping into their hamlets, engaging in dialogue, and actively listening to their concerns, she has fostered genuine connections, especially with indigenous tribal communities. Her steadfast dedication fostered immense trust from the tribal community, leading to their enthusiastic participation in various initiatives. Her ability to go beyond the bureaucracy and connect with people on a personal level has made her a true advocate for their well-being. Praseetha consistently provides exposure to the outside world for tribal and other forest-dependent communities. She motivates them to participate in events and exhibitions, travel beyond their area of domicile, and take them for picnics and visits.

While the rise in forestry jobs in Kerala offers promising opportunities for women, navigating the challenges of a traditionally male-dominated field like the Forest Department can be undeniably tough. Despite facing some bureaucratic hurdles, resistance, and occasional setbacks her passion for her work remains undimmed. The fresh scent of the forest air and the genuine appreciation and love of the tribal communities serve as her constant source of motivation, propelling her forward.

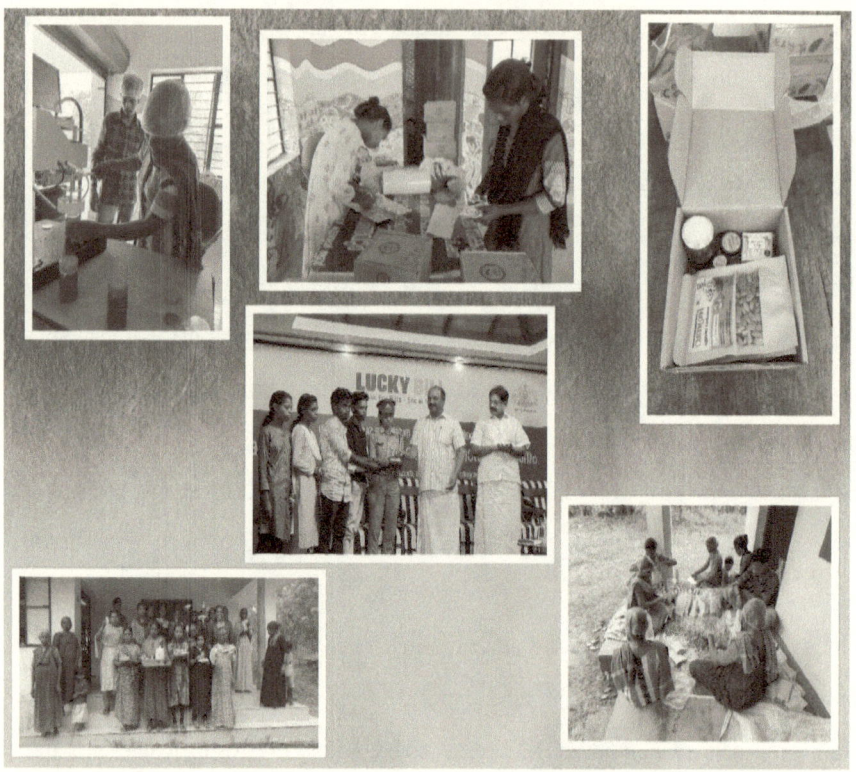

Empowering Lives: A Look at Livelihood Activities within the Chalakudy Forest Division's PFM Program.

Chapter – 2

'Punarjeevanam': The Indigenous Millet Conservation Project in Anamudi

Millets are a group of small-grained cereal grasses that offer high nutritional value and can thrive under challenging conditions. Despite their potential, millets are not widely consumed. Millets can be classified into two main categories based on grain size: major millets and small grain millets. (Gowri and Shivakumar, 2020).

Major millets include sorghum and pearl millet, while small grain millets encompass finger millet, foxtail millet, kodo millet, proso millet, barnyard millet, and little millet. Compared to rice and wheat, millets boast a richer profile of minerals and vitamins. These nutritious grains hold immense potential to enhance food security, nutrition, animal feed, fiber production, health promotion, livelihood opportunities, and ecological well-being. (*ibid*).

'Punarjeevanam', the project for conserving indigenous millet varieties and other traditional agriculture varieties cultivated by the indigenous tribal communities was launched by the Anamudi FDA (Munnar Wildlife Division & Chinnar Wildlife Sanctuary) in 2015-16. The Punarjeevanam project aims to revive and increase the cultivation of rare and endemic millet varieties in the tribal colonies of Marayoor-Anchunadu. Through strict organic cultivation, the project has been successful in retrieving and conserving over 35 varieties of millets, 16 varieties of beans, and other ethnic agricultural varieties in the past few years.

In the first phase, 8 varieties of ethnic ragi (finger millet) were restored. In the second phase, 15 varieties of ragi were restored, and by the end of the third phase, the number of varieties of millets that had been restored had reached 21. In addition to ragi, through the project, the Forest Department has restored ethnic varieties of beans, pumpkin, amaranth, maize, and other traditional agriculture varieties. In the fourth

45

phase of the project, 26 varieties of finger millets were restored, and 21 varieties of beans were cultivated.

The millet conservation project was first implemented in Thayannankudy, one of the Muthuvan Tribal settlements in Chinnar Wildlife Sanctuary. Thayannankudy Eco-development Committee (EDC) was given the responsibility to launch and manage the project. The members of the EDC gathered rare millet varieties from various nearby tribal colonies. Fifteen cents of land was leased by the EDC from the farmers of those colonies for the project.

From the fourth phase onwards, the Punarjeevanam program was also extended to two more tribal colonies (Eachampetty and Iruttalakudy). In the fifth phase of the project, 30 varieties of ragi were collected and cultivated; the same was done in the other two colonies mentioned earlier. In the sixth phase, 31 varieties of ragi were restored. In the second stage of the sixth phase, beans were also cultivated. In the first stage of the seventh phase, 35 varieties of ragi have been restored.

The Kerala Agriculture Department has given due recognition to the project. The Thayannankudy EDC was chosen and awarded as the best tribal community in the state for its outstanding efforts in preserving traditional agricultural practices in partnership with the Forest Department. The Punarjeevanam project was awarded by the Global Environmental Council (World Malayalee Council) as the best project for conserving biodiversity in Kerala in 2018. In the same year, the project received the prestigious national-level Plant Genome Savior Award. The project was also honoured with the Indian Biodiversity Award 2021, a certificate of appreciation for the conservation of domesticated species.

Through the Punarjeevanam project, the Anamudi FDA aims to revive and expand traditional farming practices in more than 25 tribal colonies in and around the Marayoor-Kanthalloor region and to elevate the area as a hub of ethnic millet production in Kerala.

The Regional Overview of Food Security and Nutrition 2023 report by The Food and Agriculture Organization (FAO) states that 74.1 percent of Indians were unable to afford a healthy diet in 2021 and 16.6 percent of India's population was undernourished from 2020–2022 which was a major national concern. In this context, cultivating and consuming millets emerges as a powerful solution to address nutrient deficiencies in the population.

The Warriors of Punarjeevanam Project in Anamudi.

Chapter – 3

'Unarvu' in Silent Valley

Silent Valley

Located in the Nilgiri hills of Kerala, in the Nilgiri Biosphere Reserve, Silent Valley National Park is home to a variety of rare species of flora and fauna, including the lion-tailed macaque, the Nilgiri Thar, and the sholas. (Parameswaran, 1979). It is a UNESCO World Heritage Site surrounded by other protected areas, including the Karimpuzha Wildlife Sanctuary, the New Amarambalam Reserved Forest, and the Nedumkayam Rainforest. The Bhavani River and Kunthipuzha River originate in the vicinity of Silent Valley National Park which are important sources of water for the people. The tribal communities around Silent Valley National Park are mainly agriculturists, including the Kurumba, Muduga, and Irula tribes (Padmanabhan, 2007).

Unarvu

Envisaged by Pramod G Krishnan IFS, the Unarvu Tribal Youth and Cultural Center is situated in the Bhavani Range of the Silent Valley Forest Division in Mukkali of the Attapadi region. Unarvu is comprised of a library, cultural space, and an online facility center. Since its inception in 2016, the center has provided coaching for public service commission exams, physical training sessions for armed force recruitment, entrance to professional programs, and support for job placement. The advanced online facilities provided at Unarvu remain a great support and blessing for the tribal youth. The center organizes various sports, arts, and cultural programs. The 'Unarvu Football Fest' is a much-celebrated event and has attracted state-wide recognition. Teams constituted by the members of Eco-development Committees (EDC) compete in the tournament. During the last seven years, the majority of the tribal youth who have been undergoing training for various competitive exams have successfully cleared them and have entered government services.

The library that functions in the Center is a popular destination for students, youth, and other residents of the area. With over 3,000 books, 30 magazines, and 8 newspapers, it offers a wide variety of reading material for people of all interests. The library is also home to computers and study spaces, making it a great place to work or relax. Since there are no other libraries in the nearby area, the Unarvu library has become a vital resource for the community and offers free admission to all. It has become a great place for the members of the tribal hamlets to learn, grow, and connect with others.

Yet another initiative was completed by the Forest Department in 2017. A three-month-long driving course with the help of a private driving school in Mannarkad was provided for several tribal women in the region and a considerable number of them benefited from the project, which may be considered as 'empowerment in motion' (Satish, 2017).

Through the support received from Unarvu Center, several tribal students have secured admission to higher education in various Universities. The center continues to play a significant role in the social, cultural, and economic advancement of tribal communities. It has also ignited a passion for reading among both youngsters and adults.

Unarvu Center, a Haven of Tranquility in Silent Valley's Embrace.

Chapter – 4
Tribal Markets of Marayoor and Munnar

Marayoor

Located between Munnar and Udumalpet in Kerala, Marayoor is a scenic place of historic significance. It is home to several ancient ruins, including rock paintings and dolmens. The well-known dolmens are located in Muniyara near Kovilkadavu. They are chambers made of four stones placed on the edges and covered with a capstone. They are believed to be the burial chambers of the Stone Age people. Marayoor is also famous for the rare Neelakurunji flowers that bloom once every 12 years. It attracts a large number of visitors to the region (Forest Department, 2021)

Chilla

Chilla is an initiative launched by the Marayoor Forest Division and managed by the Periyakudi Vana Samrakshana Samiti (VSS) to ensure a market for trading NTFPs and various agricultural products from the tribal hamlets of Marayoor. The market ensures pesticide-free products to the general public. Initiated in 2014, the turnover has reached over rupees 2 crore. The Chilla market also ensures a regular income for the tribal communities and local farmers thereby reducing their dependency on the forest. The market also comprises farm produce and livestock from 40 tribal settlements in Marayoor.

Over the years, Chilla has become a major market with consumers and traders flocking from far-away destinations to take part in the auction. The tribal communities bring their produce to the market which leads to open auctions in their presence. Earlier the tribal communities sold their produce for the price mandated by private traders. However, after the introduction of the Chilla market, the goods are sold at auction. Hence the tribal communities get a better price in comparison to the previous

51

practice of heeding to the nominal price offered by private traders. Hence, Chilla has helped several tribal communities to overcome the exploitation of middlemen. Moreover, it supports nearly two hundred tribal women who are engaged in farming to earn a direct price which results in the free flow of income, and financial independence leading to their empowerment and better standards of living.

Overall, the Chilla market is a positive development for tribal communities. Apart from helping to increase their income, and improve their standard of living, it has resulted in a higher bargaining power for their produce.

Ila Supermarket

Despite the improvement in living conditions of tribal communities in Marayoor, consistent growth has remained elusive. Forest department officials conducted a thorough investigation to understand the underlying reasons for this stagnation. Through direct and indirect interactions with tribal community members, it was discovered that they are often exploited by middlemen and traders from whom they purchase daily necessities such as groceries and food items. Tribal communities often face arduous journeys from their hamlets to Munnar and Udumalpetta in Tamil Nadu to procure these essentials. Covering these long distances and returning on the same day is an impractical task. As a result, they are compelled to rely on businesses in Marayoor. However, many of these traders exploit the situation by charging exorbitant prices for their goods, taking advantage of the tribal communities' limited access to alternatives. To address this issue and prevent exploitation, the Marayoor FDA opened the Ila supermarket with financial support from SFDA in 2022, which is a 'no-profit-no-loss' shop for tribal communities to purchase consumer goods. It was set up with a grant of Rs 10 lakhs from the State Forest Development Agency (SFDA). The store provides credit facilities to tribal farmers and protection watchers, who sell their agricultural produce in the Chilla market. The shop is open every day and is exclusively for tribal and other forest-dependent communities. SUPPLYCO provides goods to the store at a reduced rate. The initiative became an instant hit by achieving a turnover of Rs 25000/- per day. The supermarket also offers credit facilities to the tribal communities.

Munnar

Located in the Idukki District of Kerala, Munnar was a wild and unexplored landscape until the 1870s. British Resident John Daniel Munro visited the place and leased the Kanan Devan hills from the Poonjar royal family and started planting coffee, cardamom, cinchona, and sisal. Tea was found to be the ideal crop for the region which led to its plantations in 1880. In 1895, Finlay Muir & Company bought 33 independent estates and formed the Kannan Devan Hills Produce Company to manage them. The Tata Group entered the plantation business in 1964 and formed Tata Tea Ltd. in 1983. The tourism industry re-discovered Munnar in the latter half of the 20th century and it is now a popular hill station. The Munnar region has been inhabited by tribal communities such as the Malayarayan and Muthuvan, for thousands of years (Rammohan *et al.*,2015), (Dhali, 2015).

Masalappetty Tribal Market of Munnar

Following the example of the Chilla market in Marayoor, the Munnar FDA initiated a local open market called Masalappetty (Haat Bazaar) under the leadership of Ancham Mile Vana Samraksha Samithi (VSS) in May 2022 to ensure the tribal communities and local farmers in the region get a fair price for their produces. Items especially agricultural and vegetables produced from 28 tribal hamlets are traded in Masalappetty. The market provides seeds to local farmers to ensure quality. The market also sells handicrafts that are prepared by tribal communities.

Tribal communities produce high-quality goods, but they have difficulty obtaining a fair price and access to markets. Masalapetty aims to stop the exploitation of tribal people and guarantee them a fair price for their products. This open market has turned into a success story with considerable sales turnover.

Chapter – 5

The Pepper Farmers of Periyar East

Periyar

Located in Thekkady (Idukki), Periyar is one among the 27 tiger reserves in India. It was originally a hunting ground for the Travancore kings. In 1950, (post-independence) the region was declared a wildlife sanctuary. In 1978, the sanctuary was included in Project Tiger, a national initiative to protect the tiger population. In 1992, the reserve also became a part of Project Elephant, a national initiative to protect the Asian elephant population. It is home to rich wildlife, including tigers, elephants, leopards, sloth bears, and deer, and also home to rare and endangered species, such as the Nilgiri tahr and lion-tailed macaque. Periyar is a popular tourist destination and offers a variety of activities, such as elephant safaris, boat rides, and hiking. Mannans, Paliyans, Malayarayans, Mala Pandarams, Uralis, and Ulladans are the major tribal communities residing in the Periyar region (Sasidharan,1998),(Arun *et al.*, 2001).

Vanchivayal Organic Pepper

Since 2008, the tribal communities of Periyar have been exporting organic pepper to Ecoland Herbs and Spices, a German Co-operative located in Wolpertshausen (Germany). The Periyar Tiger Foundation (PTR), established in 2004, collects and grades pepper dried by the Urali families of Vanjivayal, a village inside the reserve, as part of the Participatory Forest Management (PFM) program. The first consignment of pepper to Germany was exported in April 2008. Thus the pepper from this region earned the name 'Vanchivayal Organic Pepper'. Richabel Bio Foods India Limited is involved in the collection of Pepper on behalf of Ecoland Herbs and Spices.

Pepper is cultivated on 40.2 hectares in the tribal settlements of Vanchivayal, which falls under the jurisdiction of the Vallakkadavu Forest Range of PTR. The farming area has received organic certification from the Sikkim State Organic Certification Agency which is annually renewed. The expenses for the certification are taken care of by the FDA. The procedure involves collecting organically grown pepper from farmers and then testing for quality and moisture content at the Spices Board lab. Once the samples are approved, they get ready for export to Germany. The export is only initiated after ensuring that the pepper is free of chemicals and has the right moisture content thereby assuring the highest quality.

Despite its huge potential, the pepper project has its ups and downs. In 2020 due to certain unforeseen events, the contract was not initiated by the Forest Department and the German firm. Hence, farmers had to sell the pepper for cheaper rates. However, the export picked up in due course of time.

In August 2023, the Vanchivayal tribal settlement, home to the Oorali community, was honored with the prestigious "Second Best Organic Tribal Hamlet Award" in the state. This recognition marks a remarkable achievement for the community, as it was also bestowed upon them in 2017, highlighting their unwavering commitment to sustainable agricultural practices.

The Vanchivayal model of tribal farming has attained a lot of appreciation. It ensures a 40 percent higher price in comparison to market rates. Fifty-nine farmers are involved in the farming that benefits over seventy-one families. The success of Vanjivayal has contributed a lot in uplifting the lifestyle of the tribal communities by fetching an alternative and a steady income for the tribal farmers.

Chapter – 6

Creating Knowledge Hubs, Enchasing Creativity & Introducing Space Technology in Tribal Hamlets

Mission Knowledge Project – Establishing 'Kathir' Library

In 2022, the State Forest Development Agency (SFDA) launched an initiative called "Kathir" to organize libraries, cultural, and career orientation centers for tribal hamlets in Kerala. The project aims to adopt and transform tribal hamlets into cultural and learning centers. SFDA has associated with various universities, educational institutions, NGOs, private companies, and the general public to establish the mission as a public consortium. Educational institutions have come forward to participate in the project by donating books and other logistics such as book shelfs, book registers, etc. The project aims to improve reading habits among tribal communities, especially tribal students. It also aims to motivate tribal youth to attend schools and take up higher studies to build fruitful careers. Kathir also aims to create knowledge hubs in each tribal hamlet and support tribal youth and students in skill development through training and allied activities. So far, through the Mission Knowledge Project, SFDA has established 10 Kathir libraries in various tribal hamlets across the State.

Virtual Arts Outreach Camps

SFDA has been organizing several camps on painting (Virtual Art Camps), clay modeling, counseling, and personality development for the students of various tribal communities across the state. Students lead the 'Trespassers' artist group of the Sree Sankaracharya University, Kalady spearheads the 5-day camp. Since 2020, the SFDA has organized seven camps in various districts of the State.

Opening New Frontiers of Space Technology in Tribal Hamlets

SFDA organizes science workshops in cooperation with the Indian Institute of Space Science and Technology (IIST) of the Indian Space Research Organization (ISRO) in tribal hamlets to sensitize the community members, especially the younger generation to modern scientific avenues, including rocketry and drone technology. The fun-filled camp is open to everyone in the hamlet, not just students. This is a rare opportunity for the community, so they make the most of it. Telescope viewing and rocket launching are just a few of the activities that everyone enjoys, as these are experiences that they rarely get to have.

The first camp titled 'Arivanka Karumam' was held from 31st December 2022 to 2nd January 2023 in Thenmala with the participation of 60 school students and members of the Kanikkar tribal hamlet of Villumala (Thenmala Forest Division). This camp received national media coverage (front page coverage in Hindu Daily dated 03-01-2023). The second camp titled 'Jolsana' was held in Chalakudy Forest Division with the participation of over a hundred students from the Kadar tribal community.

The Virtual art camp and IIST workshop have become a major event for the entire hamlet, not just for children. Participation is not limited to young people, and the residents welcome these camps with open arms. During a camp in Thenmala, the entire village gathered at a nearby school to gaze at the stars through telescopes. They celebrated the gathering as a grand festival.

The collaboration between the Forest Department and various external organizations exemplifies the power of partnerships in addressing societal challenges and promoting sustainable development. By working together, these organizations are empowering tribal youth and fostering a culture of scientific inquiry and talent development among the forest-dependent communities.

Outreach Programs Have a Deep and Positive Impact on the Lives of the Less Privileged

Reader's attention is invited to a small, but significant incident that occurred during one of the Drishykala Outreach camps organized by the SFDA, titled "Onkal" hosted by Vachumaram VSS in Vazhachal FDA. On the first day of the camp, one of the participants informed the PFM Manager that a handicapped boy who could not walk or speak would like to join the camp. PFM Manager and the rest of the camp organizers went to the boy's house, helped him bathe and get ready, and brought him to the camp.

The boy interacted with the other children despite his challenges. He drew pictures, made clay models, and participated in other activities in which he was able to take part. On the last day of the camp, he was awarded a certificate of participation along with the other participants. Out of overwhelming emotions, he could not speak, instead, he expressed his gratitude to the PFM Manager by taking his hands and crying. It was an emotional moment for both of them. The boy's tears of joy showed how much the camp and the certificate meant to him. Those may have been among his most prized possessions. Such gestures benefit people, especially those who are deprived of opportunities in life. They also play a crucial role in binding the forest-dependent communities with the Forest Department.

Outreach programs play a crucial role in empowering forest-dependent communities, particularly their youth, to adapt to a changing society. These programs act as bridges, fostering connections both within the community and with the outside world. Despite modern advancements and shifting lifestyles, many tribal hamlets remain isolated from mainstream society. Outreach programs can bridge this gap, exposing them to new perspectives and opportunities. They also present an invaluable chance for the Forest Department to strengthen its relationship with these communities.

Quantitative Aspects v/s Human Dimension

The attraction of quantitative aspects like infrastructure development often blinds certain bureaucrats to the vital role qualitative outreach programs play in empowering forest-dependent communities, especially through Participatory Forestry Management (PFM) initiatives. These rigid, old-school mindsets, clinging to the outdated notion of forest protection as the sole objective, fail to grasp the transformative potential of qualitative approaches. While forest protection remains paramount, it cannot be a solitary shield against the radical shifts shaking society.

Forest leadership needs an evolutionary leap, embracing a holistic approach that balances quantitative and qualitative methods. Building bridges through outreach programs, fostering connections within and beyond communities, and empowering youth through experiential learning are not soft luxuries, but strategic investments in the future of forests. These programs cultivate a sense of ownership, foster sustainable resource management practices, and equip communities to become active stewards of their environment. Ignoring their value is akin to building a fortress without a foundation, leaving the forest vulnerable to the very forces we seek to protect.

It's high time for a paradigm shift in forest management to move beyond the sterile confines of quantitative metrics and embrace the human dimension. By nurturing the hearts and minds of those who call the forest home, the Forest Department engages to build a resilient shield against external threats and cultivate a future where people and nature thrive in harmony.

A Look at the Outreach Programs.

Chapter – 7

From Alcoholism to Football: The Case of Kadar Community in Chalakudy

Alcohol use is widespread in numerous cultures and across regions (WHO, 2019). Substance abuse is a major problem in tribal hamlets across the state. Marginalized communities (tribes, economically or socially deprived communities) are often victims of the harmful effects of alcohol (Shihab,2020). The use of substances and dependence on alcohol have increased drastically among tribal communities in recent years (Sadath *et al.*,2023). People of all ages are now victims of substance abuse and alcohol. This has led to a rise in domestic violence, school dropouts, health problems, and deaths. Tackling substance abuse has become a daunting challenge for the government authorities.

The Chalakudy Initiative

Thrissur district is a significant consumer of alcohol in Kerala, ranking third in overall consumption within the state. This is further evident by the presence of three of the top 10 Kerala State Beverages Corporation Ltd (BEVCO) outlets in the Thrissur district. (Ullas, 2012). Notably, Chalakudy stands in sixth position in the state for liquor sales through BEVCO outlets as of 2023.

The influence of alcohol has a detrimental impact on tribal communities in Chalakudy, leading to a range of negative consequences that can disrupt social harmony and hinder overall well-being. Many tribal youth from the Kadar community are found wandering and resorting to alcohol and smoking. The major part of the income earned by them through the collection and sales of NTFPs is spent on alcoholic drinks and cigarettes. NTFP collectors among tribal communities often sell their forest produce at a loss or even give it away for free to private parties just to get a bottle of alcohol or a packet of cigarettes. Awareness classes and other training programs have proved to be useful, but they have limitations in having a lasting impact on the community. Considering the situation, under the leadership of Praseeda E P (PFM Coordinator, Chalakudy FDA), and with the guidance and support of the Divisional Forest Officer (DFO) the members of Anapaantham Tribal VSS have initiated a unique method to tackle alcoholism and substance abuse: engaging in various sport activities.

A nearby ground within the tribal hamlet was chosen as the playground. Excited by the prospect, the male tribal youth purchased a football and started playing. Every evening, instead of roaming, they would gather near the ground to play football. Inspired by the men, the women members of the community are also engaged in various sports. Gradually, the tribal community in Anapaantham is in the process of refocusing itself from alcohol to sports.

While this may seem like a small project, such social initiatives have a profound impact on forest-dependent communities, particularly empowering tribal youth to reshape their futures and equipping them to face life's challenges.

Youngsters of the Kadar Tribal Community are Seen Engaging in Sports.

Chapter – 8

The 'Mancode' Model of Development

As Participatory Forestry activities in Kerala cross twenty-five years, the exemplary work of ABP Wildlife Division's Mancode Eco-Development Committee (EDC) deserves special attention. Mancode EDC is located within the Neyyar-Peppara FDA of ABP Wildlife, in Thiruvananthapuram. The fact that Mancode EDC's activities are centered on the local tribal community (Kani) is commendable in every way. The EDC has been engaging in exemplary work by raising funds through unique means. It is worth mentioning that the operations of this EDC remain self-funded and acquired from various donors (Alexander, 2021).

Vanika Project

Perhaps Vanika is a model project that can be emulated by all PFM institutions in Kerala. Several activities have been carried out by this EDC in Mancode through this project. In the context of COVID-19, the crops grown by the tribal communities were delivered to the needy with the help of publicity on social media platforms, thereby getting a good price for the local cultivators. In addition, it was possible to provide the necessary materials to the tribal villages. Temporary food units were started to implement the scheme. Honey, cashew, tamarind, tapioca, turmeric, lemon, lentil, sorghum, yam, plantain, mango, guava, and pepper were successfully marketed. Through the Vanika Project, various types of pickles to community kitchens were distributed free of cost during the lockdown period. Through the program called Vanika Smart Challenge, online classes were provided to tribal students through the Kite Victors channel using smartphones.

Community Farming

Mancode EDC strongly supports the efforts of tribal communities to revive the farming tradition of the Kotoor region. Many tribal families who prepared traditional agricultural land were able to reap good harvests. With the cooperation provided by the Forest Department, it was possible to ensure the participation of tribal youth in agriculture. Additionally, agriculture-related training is also provided. With the help of the Forest Department, the members of Mancode EDC have been distributed farming equipments such as pickaxes and shovels. This proved to be of great help to many families and increased their interest in agriculture.

Kani Chantha (Auction Market)

The Mancode EDC organizes a weekly auction market to sell crops grown by the tribal communities. The Mancode Community Center is used to organize the auction market. One of the main objectives of this initiative is to avoid exploitation by middlemen. Bidding is only allowed above the support price to ensure better prices for the crops. The auction market is also called Kani Chantha, which means "market of the Kani tribe". "Kani" means "tribal community in the region" and "chantha" means "market". The auction market is a place where the Kani tribe members auction off their produce, such as honey, coffee, and spices.

Other Community Welfare Activities

Skill development, written tests, interview tests, and skill training for Public Service Commission (PSC) exams are conducted free of cost to the students of the tribal community. The activities of Macode EDC have become a shelter for many youths in tribal hamlets. In yet another initiative, beehives were distributed to selected tribal families with the help of the College of Agriculture, Vellayani. In addition, more than sixty training programs were organized. In association with the Central Tuber

Crop Research Institute (CTCRI), a project was developed for tuber cultivation, valued at thirty thousand rupees. Thirteen selected families have benefited from this scheme. As part of the COVID-19 management, a portion of the profit from the sale of forest products was used to distribute Rs 10,000 and 250 masks to students at a government school for the visually impaired in Jagati, Thiruvananthapuram. In association with companies in Technopark Park in Thiruvananthapuram, Mancode EDC is providing a scholarship of Rs. 5,000 to selected underprivileged children from the Kani tribal community. This scholarship is provided until they acquire a job. Kunjata is a short film released at the beginning of the COVID-19 era under the leadership of Mancode EDC with the support of the Kerala Forest Department. Through this short film, awareness was created among the local people about the use of masks and sanitizers. During the COVID-19 era, Mancode EDC, in collaboration with Kattakada Christian College, distributed food kits to tribal communities, which became a model for many others to follow.

Circle Asst. PFM Coordinator Sinukumar, Division PFM Coordinator Sajjayan, and Mancode EDC Secretary Gopika Surendran were at the forefront of these initiatives. The generous assistance of Shri. J. R. Ani, Wildlife Warden, has been a great asset to the activities of the EDC. The organized nature of the Mancode EDC members continues to be a good model for PFM activities through the involvement of the forest tribal communities and by carrying out innovative activities. Through PFM, Mancode EDC continues to play its part in forest protection and strengthening the livelihoods of forest-dwelling communities, thereby reducing deforestation through grassroots-level participatory activities.

Chapter – 9

Indigenous Food Festivals

Humans need a variety of nutrients to maintain good health. These nutrients can only be obtained through a balanced diet. The amount of nutrients a person needs depends on their age, gender, health status, and activity level. It is worth noting that tribal cuisines are an important part of Kerala's cultural and culinary heritage (Geroge *et al.,* 2017). Forests are crucial for enhancing the food security of tribal communities. Wild edible plants play a significant role in the subsistence strategies of forest dwellers and tribal populations (Yesodharan & Sujana, 2007). Each tribal community has its unique cuisine and they use fresh, local ingredients, many of which are wild or grown in traditional ways. They are very healthy, as it features a variety of fruits, vegetables, and whole grains that are fresh, and locally available. Moreover, these cuisines are rich in nutritional value, and a part of the cultural identity of the State that showcases the rich biodiversity and the traditional knowledge of its tribal communities. They have a deep understanding of the natural world and prepare food in a sustainable manner that in turn protects the environment. Tribal cuisines are well known for their unique cooking methods and flavours. Many of these dishes are often seasoned with a variety of wild herbs and spices and they are cooked in bamboo or earthen pots, which gives them a distinctive flavour. The potential of indigenous cuisines as a significant economic opportunity for tribal communities deserves exploration, especially given today's growing demand for fresh, unadulterated food.

Indigenous Food Festival in Trivandrum

Ponmudi VSS, with the support from Trivandrum FDA and USAID's Forest-PLUS 2.0 program, organized a Food Festival in April 2022 serving the indigenous food of the Kani tribal community. As inhabitants of the Agasthyamala

Biosphere Reserve, the community's deep understanding of the local flora is critical to the management and conservation of these vast forests.

Some of the unique cuisines like Parandakka Payasam, Arogya-paccha Juice, Mathenga Payasam, Kumbalappam, and Narunandi Sarbath along with other traditional food items were served to the visitors and the public. The community also managed to avoid wasting any food due to their meticulous planning. Moreover, they served the food on arrowroot leaves, making the event sustainable in every way.

Indigenous Millet Festival in Chalakudy

The Chalakudy FDA organized two food festivals in response to the International Year of Millets (2023). The first event, titled "Millet Festival," was held from December 31, 2022, to January 1, 2023. Millet kheer (payasam) prepared by women members of the Kaarikadavu Tribal Hamlet using foxtail millet, little millet (sourced from Attappadi tribal hamlets) were distributed. One glass of Kheer was sold for Rs. 20 which turned out to be a success. The second event was held on April 17, 2023, as part of the Vana Sauhridha Sadhasu. The women members of the Kaarikadavu Tribal Hamlet prepared and distributed bamboo seeds and chama kheer. Nearly 300 members, including Sri. A. K. Saseendran, the Honorable Forest Minister of Kerala, tasted the food and appreciated their efforts. The FDA could also secure bulk orders from the participants.

Food festivals are much more than just cooking. Tribal women were involved in a considerable number of activities, such as event management, food presentation, accounting, collecting raw materials, coordinating events, and managing a large crowd. This has instilled a lot of confidence in them. Organizing ethnic food festivals regularly offers a unique opportunity to promote the nutrient-rich culinary traditions of tribal communities in the State on a larger scale, helping to preserve their food systems. It is also an opportunity to introduce and interconnect tribal communities and their cultural and culinary heritage with the urban population.

The National Family Health Survey for 2019-20 stated that Kerala's obesity rate surpasses the national average. The survey found that 38.1 percent of women and 36.4 percent of men from Kerala in the age group of 15 to 49 years were obese. Considering the dire situation, it would be worthwhile to promote healthy indigenous cuisines. Since the tribal communities in Kerala offer a range of healthy cuisines, they can play a vital role in building a healthy generation.

Food Festival Held in Ponmudi with the Support of Forest-PLUS 2.0.
Pic Courtesy- Forest-PLUS 2.0.

Chapter – 10

Vanasree – Food from Forest

Non-timber forest products (NTFPs) encompass a diverse range of plant and animal resources harvested from forests. Despite their significant economic value, these products often go unrecorded in national economies (Shiva, 1995). The Western Ghats are a treasure trove of NTFPs (Sreenivasan *et al.*, 2005). NTFP-yielding plants in the Western Ghats constituted about 40 percent of the flora (Muraleedharan *et al.*,2005). More than 150 NTFPs, including medicinal plants, edible fruits, leaves, and different types of honey, are collected from the forests of Kerala by tribal communities (Alex & Vidyasagaran, 2016).

The collection of NTFPs has helped to alleviate poverty and improve the standard of living of forest-dwelling communities(Talukdar *et al.*,2021) By selling NTFPs to markets, tribal communities are able to earn additional income and generate sustainable livelihoods(Gopinath *et al.*,2022).

A Brief History

The state established an organized marketing channel for NTFPs by setting up a chain of tribal service cooperative societies. These societies are federated at the state level with the Kerala State Federation of Scheduled Caste and Scheduled Tribes Development Co-operative Ltd., which was established in 1981. However, in 1991, the state discontinued the system of royalty for NTFPs collected by tribal communities. It took another one and a half decades for the Forest Rights Act of 2006 to be passed, which conferred ownership rights of NTFPs on tribal communities. Hence, presently only tribal communities are allowed to collect NTFPs.

The Role of PFM in NTFP Management

PFM has opened up new opportunities for forest-dependent tribal communities in Kerala. Since the inception of PFM in Kerala, the livelihood improvement of tribes has become a priority. In 2002, an institutional mechanism with adequate financial support was initiated for the management of NTFPs collected by tribal communities. Scientific stock assessment in the wild, sustainable collection, proper storage, value addition, and marketing of NTFPs were identified as the keys to tribal livelihood. Some of the tribal service cooperative societies took the lead in marketing products like wild honey, black dammar, and wild turmeric. The response to these products was overwhelming, which prompted the Forest Department to consider a formal value addition and marketing chain. This led to the establishment of Vanasree, a unique venture established by the Kerala Forest and Wildlife Department under the SFDA for the management and sale of NTFPs collected by the indigenous tribal forest-dependent communities.

Vanasree, as an initiative of the Kerala Forest Department, over the past decades has played a significant role in empowering tribal communities and promoting the sustainable use of NTFPs. Vanasree as a brand was established in 2010 under the leadership of SFDA to provide better market access and prices to NTFPs collected by the tribal communities by eliminating the exploitation by middlemen. The NTFPs collected by the tribal communities are processed, value-added with the participation of the tribal community, and sold through Vanasree outlets. The Vanasree mechanism provides support to tribal communities to collect, process, and market NTFPs in a sustainable manner. This has helped to improve the quality and marketability of NTFPs and has resulted in higher incomes for tribal communities. The Vanasree mechanism has also helped to raise awareness about the importance of NTFPs and the need for sustainable forest management. Also, by providing technical support on sustainable harvesting protocols, Vanasree is helping to protect the forests of Kerala and the livelihoods of tribal communities.

Currently, 72 Vanasree outlets are operating under 36 FDAs in the State. Through these outlets, the Forest Department was able to sell NTFPs worth Rs. 7,520,191,1/- in 2022-2023 (financial year). The revenue generated is entirely used by the Forest Department for the upliftment of the indigenous forest-dependent tribal communities. By understanding the availability of NTFPs in each forest, the Forest Divisions are able to conserve and sustain them and implement the necessary regeneration processes.

The Forest Department markets the best forest resources available in the country through Vanasree. The Department is involved in the marketing of about 50 forest products, such as honey, turmeric, black pepper, tamarind, aquatic rotula, cutch, musk turmeric, bamboo seed, ginger, gooseberry, acacia wild, etc., from the inner forests of the Western Ghats. In Kerala, about 50,000 forest-dependent tribal people earn their livelihood through NTFP collection. In collaboration with the Forest Department, universities, and other voluntary organizations, FDAs provide training for the scientific collection, processing, and value addition of NTFPs.

The Kerala Forest Department has launched an online marketing platform (Vanasree.in) for Vanasree products, making it easier for customers to purchase high-quality forest products from the comfort of their own homes. Vanasree products are in demand all over the country, and the revenue generated from online sales is also used to support the upliftment of tribal communities. The online marketing of Vanasree products is a welcome initiative that supports tribal communities by providing them with additional income by creating an opportunity to sell NTFPs beyond the borders of Kerala.

The Vanasree initiative, spearheaded by the Kerala Forest Department, has played a pivotal role in empowering tribal communities and promoting the sustainable utilization of non-timber forest products (NTFPs). Through PFM, the indigenous forest-dependent tribal communities have been granted extensive rights and responsibilities over the forests they inhabit. These rights encompass the collection and sale of NTFPs, active participation in forest planning and management, and the ability to reap the benefits of sustainable forest resource utilization.

The Vanasree mechanism provides comprehensive support (technical and logistics) to tribal communities in the collection, processing, and marketing of NTFPs in an environmentally responsible manner. This assistance has led to a marked improvement in the quality and marketability of NTFPs, consequently translating into higher incomes for tribal communities. The initiative has fostered a sense of ownership and responsibility among tribal members, encouraging them to become active stewards of their forest resources.

The Vanasree initiative stands as a testament to the transformative power of sustainable forest management practices. By empowering tribal communities and promoting the responsible use of NTFPs, the Vanasree mechanism has not only improved livelihoods but also continues to contribute to the conservation of Kerala's rich biodiversity.

Some of the NTFPs and Other Products Sold through Vanasree Outlets.

Chapter – 11

Kerala Forest Ecotourism:

Protecting Nature and Promoting Sustainable Tourism

The term ecotourism emerged in the late 1980s as a direct result of the world's acknowledgment and reaction to sustainable practices and global ecological practices (Weaver & Lawton, 2007). Ecotourism is responsible tourism centered on nature with an educational component, involves development that contributes to the participation and well-being of the local communities, contributes to the protection of nature, and is ecologically sustainable (Fennell, 2014). The National Geographic Magazine has labeled Kerala a paradise for tourism (Edward & George, 2008). The State has a recorded forest area of 11524.149 sq. km. Moreover, Kerala is home to 14 wildlife sanctuaries, two tiger reserves, and 6 national parks (Kerala Forest Statistics, 2020). The potential for the development of ecotourism in Kerala remains immense and can be tapped sustainably in economic terms as well as for the full benefit of the local forest-dependent communities.

The Kerala Forest Department has been involved in the management of ecotourism projects for the past 25 years (Administration Report, 2021). Even though tourism programs existed in areas like Periyar from the 1970s, the concept of ecotourism was taken up by the Kerala Forest Department in the late 90s. Ecotourism is implemented by the government of Kerala through the PFM program of the Kerala Forest Department. Detailed guidelines for the management of ecotourism centers have been issued by the Government vide Government Order No.18/2002 dated 02-04-2002. Similarly, for providing financial assistance to ecotourism destinations by the Tourism Department, detailed guidelines have been issued vide Government Order No.3314/2009 dated 30-04-2005.

Kerala Forest Ecotourism operates 213 packages throughout the State, including Wildlife sanctuaries and National Parks. These packages are operated under 71 ecotourism centers within 33 FDAs with the participation of 93 VSS/EDC (PFM Institutions). The principal ecotourism products of the Kerala Forest Department can be classified into 8 categories namely (1) Trekking (2) Staying (3) Site Seeing (4) Safari (5) Boating (6) Waterfalls (7) Camping and (8) others.

Salient Features of Kerala Forest Ecotourism

Visitors are charged an entry fee, parking fee, photography fee, and videography fee depending upon the nature of packages and facilities provided at ecotourism centers. This is based on the concept "polluter pays principle" meaning that visitors are responsible for the environmental impact of their activities. This helps to ensure that the ecotourism centers are sustainable and do not damage the environment. The money (visitor fee) is collected as the Eco-system Management Fund (EMF) and it is used to maintain the ecotourism centers, and rural development, protect the environment, and pay wages to people engaged in respective ecotourism centers. The Kerala Forest Ecotourism engages over 2100 forest-dependent persons as guides and caretakers who are the direct beneficiaries of the project. The department has established Vanasree eco shops in most of the ecotourism centers to sell value-added NTFPs thereby creating additional employment opportunities for the forest-dependent communities. Moreover, the forest department also provides insurance coverage to all visitors to ecotourism destinations, except foreigners. The forest-dependent communities who are engaged in the management of ecotourism centers are also covered under the insurance scheme.

PFM, Ecotourism, and Local Community Participation

The ecotourism program managed by the Kerala Forest Department is executed through the Participatory Forest Management (PFM) program and managed by native people through PFM institutions (VSS/EDC) under the direct supervision of FDAs. This ensures the full participation of the local communities (forest-dependent communities) who are members of PFM institutions (VSS/EDC). Usually, a VSS or EDC is engaged in the management of ecotourism centers. Some of the FDAs have created federation VSS/EDC to exclusively manage ecotourism, especially in areas with a considerable number of forest-dependent communities to guarantee the representation of various tribal and non-tribal members. Such an arrangement ensures the full participation of local forest-dependent and tribal communities in the management of ecotourism centers and provides increased opportunities for forest-dependent communities to earn a regular livelihood from ecotourism activities.

Ecosystem Management Fund (EMF) for Community Welfare and Development

The Ecosystem Management Fund (EMF) is generated from the service charges collected from visitors in the Ecotourism centers carried out by VSS/EDC in the forest areas. EMF is divided on a proportion of 90:10 between FDAs and the SFDA. Out of the 70 percent share retained by FDAs, 40 percent has been allocated for implementing various activities and projects for the welfare of the local communities, 10 percent is allocated for forest protection, 15 percent is utilized for management and maintenance of ecotourism centers, whereas 4 percent is to be utilized for promoting environmental awareness and 1 percent is retained as 'flexi' fund with the CEO (Divisional Forest Officer) of the FDA. The 10 percent share of SFDA is maintained as the centralized fund which is returned to the FDAs for various ecotourism activities and community development upon the submission of proposals.

Benefits to the Local Forest-Depended Communities

Over the past 25 years, Kerala Forest Ecotourism has created alternative livelihoods for forest-dependent communities by engaging them as guiding experts, caretakers, and sellers of value-added NTFPs. It has helped to a great extent to reduce poverty and improve the lives of these communities by providing them with a stable source of income. Ecotourism has improved the welfare of local communities by providing them with access to education, healthcare, and other essential services. It has helped in establishing a sustainable image for the state by promoting ecotourism as a way to conserve the environment and improve the lives of local people. Skill enhancement of those involved in ecotourism is yet another achievement. This is achieved through training in various areas, such as guiding, customer management, soft skills, interpretation, and first aid. This has helped to improve the quality of the ecotourism experience. Over 700 women are engaged in the ecotourism sector in the State thereby providing them with an increased opportunity for consistent earning.

Addressing Challenges and the Quest for Improvement

A considerable number of challenges need to be addressed in the management of ecotourism centers in Kerala. Priority should be given to regular training in customer service for forest officers involved in the management of ecotourism destinations. Waste management should also be given a higher priority. Another important aspect is to prioritize low-impact structures in all ecotourism centers. Promoting ethnic cuisines, opening restaurants/food courts, and organizing ethnic food festivals in major ecotourism centers can generate additional income for forest-dependent communities. Designing custom-made ecotourism packages to learn more about the environment, community, and culture of the destination (e.g., bird watching, hiking, wildlife tours, and research) will be an added advantage. This will differentiate the ecotourism offering from other tourism offerings and can attract visitors who are interested in more than just sightseeing. Grading destinations, conducting effective carrying capacity studies in all destinations, implementing security audits and certifications, and establishing comprehensive ecotourism guidelines are indeed crucial areas of concern for the overall development and sustainability of the forest ecotourism program in Kerala. These measures are essential for ensuring that ecotourism in the state is conducted responsibly and sustainably, minimizing any negative impacts on the environment and local communities. The Government of Kerala is in the process of creating an Ecotourism Authority (Directorate) which is expected to professionalize and enhance the quality of facilities and services provided at ecotourism centers.

One of the cornerstones of ecotourism is the use of sustainable materials in infrastructure development. This principle, however, often gets sidelined in favour of concrete structures, overlooking the detrimental impact on the environment. While opening new ecotourism destinations can be tempting for economic reasons, it's crucial to remember the true essence of ecotourism. It's not about maximizing profit but about sustainably managing existing structures and protecting the surrounding areas leading to the conservation of forests. Building massive concrete gates and facilities goes against the core principle of minimizing environmental impact. Instead, ecotourism should embrace sustainable materials like bamboo and other sustainable materials, ensuring both functionality and environmental responsibility by minimizing ecological damage. Ecotourism transcends mere commercial activity. It's a platform for visitors to connect with nature responsibly, gaining insights into the local ecosystem and culture, and contributing to the well-being of the community. Fees collected are not simply revenue streams, but resources for the overall welfare of the environment and the local people. Ecotourism is about more than just profit; it's about creating a sustainable and harmonious existence within natural ecosystems. The true essence of ecotourism lies in fostering a connection between visitors and the destination. It's about cherishing the beauty and cultural richness of the place, understanding its unique aspects, and actively contributing to its preservation. This deeper connection is what sets ecotourism apart from conventional tourism, emphasizing sustainability and responsible interaction with nature and the local community. There are several arguments regarding the expansion of ecotourism centers in forests. Foresters, environmentalists, green activists, politicians, and ecotourism enthusiasts all have differing viewpoints. Some argue that all ecotourism centers should be closed, and forests should be entirely off-limits to such activities. Others believe more areas should be opened for responsible forest ecotourism. Still, another group advocates for strengthening existing centers rather than opening new ones. A delicate balance between sustainability and commercial activity is essential for the future of ecotourism and the protection of our natural world.

Despite the challenges, for the past two and a half decades, the ecotourism project managed by KFD in the State has remained focused on minimizing environmental impact, raising environmental awareness, and providing benefits to conservation and local communities which is designed to venerate and protect local cultures. It has strived to improve the local economies through the creation of jobs, benefiting local businesses and local producers. The ecotourism has also benefited NTFP collectors, artisans, and other small-scale industries and continues to provide a reliable source of alternative income for forest-dependent communities, especially the tribal communities. Through the ecotourism project, the local communities are provided with a chance to showcase and preserve their local history and culture. They have also become an important part of decision-making in the management of ecotourism centers through PFM. The project has contributed to raising considerable awareness of the importance of conservation and sustainable management of tourism among the local communities and visitors in the State. The Ecotourism project consistently delivers positive benefits to the local economy, the livelihoods of local people, and environmental awareness, making it more sustainable and beneficial for all involved.

In the heart of Periyar National Park, an Enthusiastic Ecotourism Guide Passionately Shares Insights with a Group of Captivated Tourists.

Chapter – 12

The Grasslands of Pampadum Shola

Grasses, often overlooked, are essential for ecosystems. They provide a foundation for other species, retain moisture, support microorganisms, and are hotspots of biodiversity (Mendes, 2021). They are one of the major ecosystems of the world, covering close to one-third of the Earth's terrestrial surface (Squires *et al.*,2018). They have played an important role in people's livelihoods for millennia as areas producing fodder for animals. Grasslands not only have a local importance for the maintenance of biodiversity and food production, but they also affect ecological processes at the landscape level (Gaujouret al., 2012). Nevertheless, they have been declining worldwide over the past century due to a variety of factors (Egoh *et al.*, 2016).

In an anticipatory step towards curbing human-animal conflict, the Munnar Wildlife Division (Anamudi) launched a project to restore nearly 50 hectares of land in Pazhathottam that was destroyed in a forest fire in 2019. The FDA constituted an Eco-Development Committee (EDC) called Harithavasantham to spearhead the project. This EDC is the first of its kind constituted in India for eco-restoration.

The EDC members first uprooted the stumps of the burnt trees and then planted grass in the area. It also involved the clearing of invasive species of trees and planting native grasses. In the first year, 15 hectares of land were converted into grassland, and in the following two years, 20 hectares of land each were converted. As a result, they have converted a nearly 50-hectare park filled with exotic species of trees (wattle and eucalyptus) into forest land and a lush green haven teeming with wildlife. This eco-restoration project implemented in collaboration with the United Nations Development Programme (UNDP) has restored the habitat destroyed due to human intervention. Vattavada now boasts green meadows with varied habitats, thanks to the restoration efforts of the Harithavasantham EDC. With the return of the grasslands, small streams have been regenerated. Animals and birds have also begun to reappear in the area. As a result of their efforts, a new ecosystem has emerged in the region.

At present, an eco-tourism project has also been started in the area that has been converted into grasslands. Four families could be accommodated in eco-tourism cottages that have been built in a completely natural way. The Forest Department is also conducting a special 3-hour trekking program through the grasslands. EDC members are now taking note of invasive plants growing in many areas of the existing grasslands apart from maintaining the grasslands. Moreover, the income from eco-tourism is utilized for the protection of grasslands. The project has turned out to be a success, and it has helped in restoring degraded ecosystems and improve biodiversity in the area. It is a model for other eco-restoration projects across the country as well.

Chapter – 13

Medicinal Plants Project in Marayoor

Marayoor is well known for Sandalwood Forest. It is the largest natural patch of sandalwood forests in India Sandalwood from Marayoor Forest in Kerala is renowned for its exceptional quality (Shahapurmath & Hanumatha,2015). It is located between the Anaimalai, Kannan Devan, and Palani Hills on the eastern slope of the Western Ghats. The region receives low rainfall, ranging from 1000 to 1500 mm annually (Census,2011). This unique forest is home to over 65,000 sandalwood trees, which are known for their high quality and high oil content. Marayoor Jaggery is yet another famous product from Marayoor (George, 2018). It is known for its unique flavour, aroma, and nutritional value which is prepared using traditional methods.

Kattupadavalam (*trichosanthes cucumerina*), is a medicinal plant, found in Marayoor which is usually collected by middlemen from tribal communities for supply to medicine manufacturers. *Trichosanthes cucumerina*, commonly known as snake gourd, viper gourd, snake tomato, or long tomato, is a versatile plant with culinary and medicinal applications. It is typically consumed as a vegetable due to its rich nutritional profile. The plant boasts an abundance of flavonoids, carotenoids, and phenolic compounds, contributing to its diverse therapeutic properties. *Trichosanthes cucumerina* holds a prominent position in Ayurvedic and Siddha medicine due to its array of medicinal benefits, including antidiabetic, hepatoprotective, cytotoxic, anti-inflammatory, and larvicidal effects (Sandhya *et al.*,2010).

The Marayoor variety *trichosanthes cucumerina* is considered of high quality and is in high demand from the pharmaceutical industry due to its bitter taste. In Marayaroor there is scope for demand-based cultivation of the species in agricultural fields by the tribal folk. No sophistication is required for the labour involved, as seed preservation and traditional know-how are employed. Tribal communities (Hill Pulaya and

Muthivan) in Marayoor have been involved in the cultivation, harvesting, and sales of *trichosanthes cucumerina* for several years. However, they were not getting a fair price for their efforts, as the profits were pocketed by middlemen. By 2010, to address this exploitation, the Marayoor FDA intervened with the following objectives:

- To wean tribal communities away from illicit activities affecting sandalwood areas.

- To overcome poor market connectivity and ensure that tribal communities receive a larger share of the sale value.

- To prevent adulteration with other similar herbs.

- To optimize the income of tribal communities by facilitating marketing.

Every year in May, the FDA officials assess demand and negotiate with stakeholders. VSS guarantees a reliable supply of medicinal plants by securing commitments from cultivators. Then, the FDA agrees on production targets and prices with companies. Cultivation begins in July and August, and harvesting is done in February. VSS coordinators bundle and weigh the product in the presence of farmers, and then the bundles are brought to the centralized stocking facility arranged by the FDA. Finally, the FDA delivers the product. FDA promotes direct negotiation with stakeholder companies for effective delivery of goods, ensuring fair prices and assured returns. The institutional mechanism of VSS/FDA is strengthened for facilitation and to ensure quality. VSS members get the opportunity to participate in the market process, and spot cash payment results in satisfaction to stakeholders. Moreover, a part of the income is also shared between the FDA and the PFM Institutions (VSS) who are involved in the process. Kammalamkudi, Peliyakudi, Kuthukallukudi, Nellipetty, Oravayal, Cherukadavu, and Kanakkayam are the major VSS involved in the project.

The intervention by the FDA ensures stakeholder satisfaction and credibility, transparency in functioning, participatory decision-making for buyers and sellers, sustainability (aligned with the livelihood practices of the community), minimal operating costs, improved accountability and responsiveness, assurance of quality, flexibility in functioning, a model for service motive and good governance, and a steady supply of raw materials. The FDA also organizes consultative meetings for information sharing and awareness, provides continuous capacity-building programs for farmers on the mode of propagation, scientific harvesting, processing, and marketing, and provides opportunities for direct interaction.

The Intervention benefits nearly 250 families in nine Vana Samrakshan Samithis (VSS) involved in harvesting and selling *trichosanthes cucumerina*. The Marayoor FDA acts as a transitional link between PFM institutions and medicine manufacturers. The intervention by the FDA has helped to improve the lives of tribal communities in Marayoor by providing them with a fair price for their produce and helping them access new markets.

Forest Officers and a Tribal Community Member Stand by Gathered *Trichosanthes Cucumerina.*

87

Chapter – 14

Navasarani- Behind the Wheels Project in Vazhachal

Vazhachal Falls, a 100-meter-long horizontal waterfall is located in the Athirappilly Panchayath of Thrissur district. It's on the Chalakudy River (five kilometers from the Athirapally Falls) near the Vazhachal Forest Division and the Sholayar ranges. It is one of the leading ecotourism centers in the State (Forest Department, 2018).

The Navasarani Driving Project managed by the Vazhachal FDA is unique in many ways. It is a project that trains tribal communities to drive vehicles. The project was launched in August 2023 as part of a skill development program. It aims to equip 126 youngsters (above the age of 18) to be proficient in driving vehicles. Both male and female aspirants have enrolled in the driving project and it is being implemented in cooperation with the Motor Vehicles Department (MVD).

The best and most impressive part is FDA does not charge fees from the members of the tribal communities for providing them with driving lessons. The Navasarani project is funded by the Vazhachal FDA and it is being implemented in four phases.

In the first phase, FDA officials approached various tribal hamlets and generated awareness of the project. Support from secretaries of various VSS were used for this purpose and it helped the tribal communities to overcome their inhibitions. As a result, they prepared a list of members who would take part in the project. In the second phase, registration and payment of fees were completed. The participants completed the learner's test in the third phase. This phase was completed with the support of the MVD, as their instructors provided nearly ten free sessions (audio and live) to prepare candidates for the learner's test. In the final phase, the FDA aims to hand over the license to all aspirants who would complete the tests.

It is highly commendable that the Vazchacal FDA has moved away from traditional income-generation methods and embarked on a new path to empower tribal communities by strategically utilizing the untapped human potential within tribal hamlets. While driving may seem like a basic necessity like food or clothing in modern society, for tribal communities, acquiring a driving license and operating a vehicle for a living represents a significant step forward.

Given the employment opportunities in the region, the vehicle driving project will benefit the tribal communities in several ways. The place is known for ecotourism, so there is a frequent movement of visitors, food, and other items, which creates a high demand for local chauffeurs who are familiar with the terrain. Finding employment with the Vazhachal FDA and other public and private agencies also remains immense.

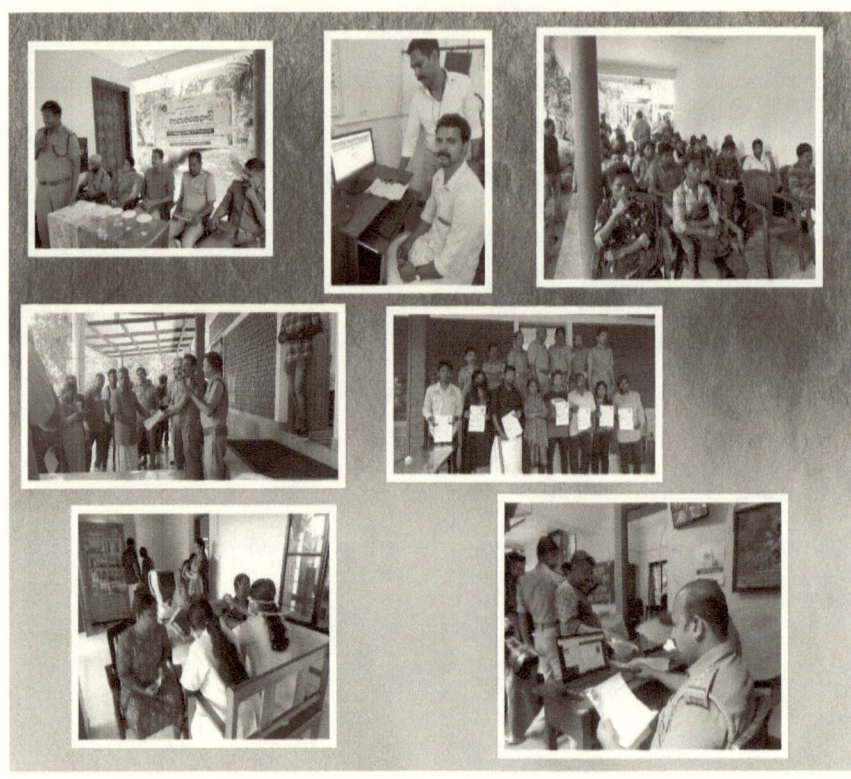

The Proceedings of the Navasarani Project in Vazhachal.

Chapter – 15

Community Services in North Wayanad

Wayanad is a hill district in northeastern Kerala, India, known for its lush green forests, cascading waterfalls, serene lakes, and abundant wildlife. It is one of the most popular tourist destinations in the state, located in the Western Ghats mountain range at an average elevation of 700 meters above sea level (Johnny, 2010). One of the main characteristics of the Wayanad district is the large aboriginal tribal population, consisting primarily of Paniyan, Adiyan, Kattunaickan, Mullu Kuruman, Urali Kuruman, and Kurichian who are distinctive in terms of culture, heritage, and living habits (Census, 2011). Interestingly, 18.5 percent of Wayanad's population comprises tribal communities which constitute 36 percent of the State's total tribal population (Issac, 2011). Wayanad is covered in dense forests, which are home to a variety of wildlife, including elephants, tigers, leopards, deer, and monkeys. The district is also home to several bird sanctuaries, which are home to a variety of migratory and resident birds (Kerala Forest Statistics, 2020). Considering this fact, the Kerala Forest Department executes a considerable amount of welfare programs through PFM.

The Jenesevana Kendram of Kunjome AVSS

The Kunjome Jenesevan Kendram (center) functions under the auspices of the Kunjome AVSS in the Periya Range of the Wayanad North FDA. It provides all the services of a government Akshaya Kendram, such as Aadhaar enrollment, ration card services, community certificates, dependency certificates, utility payments, etc.

91

Goods Hiring Shop

The goods shop is yet another initiative of the Kunjome VSS. This is a community utility shop where tribal communities can rent materials such as chairs, tables, and items for creating temporary sheds for various functions in the hamlet, like funerals, marriages, and other traditional celebrations. The items are rented out for a nominal fee or even free of cost, depending on the financial status of the renter.

Churuli Jeep Service

This service is retendered by the Churuli AVSS. Since Churuli is a large tribal colony surrounded by forests, its residents find it difficult to access schools, hospitals, and other facilities. To counter this difficulty, the leadership of the Churuli AVSS, with the support of the residents, purchased a Jeep and it is used for transporting tribal students to school, and taking patients to hospitals during emergencies, especially at odd hours.

Other Projects

The Makkimala Library was initiated by the leadership of the Makkimala AVSS. The library aims to enhance the reading habits and cultural welfare of the tribal community. Books are acquired from the public, and the library aims to affiliate with the Library Council of India in due course of time. A tailoring unit functions under the Pookodu-Cheppanam VSS, where free training programs for women are provided. Three persons are employed full-time and take up tailoring work for various government departments, especially stitching uniforms for forest watchers and the volunteers of the Panchayat Haritha Karma Sena. The members of the Papanashini VSS manage paid camps and rent out a dormitory (for a nominal fee) in Thirunelli, which provides them with daily income.

Various projects and programs executed through PFM in North Wayanad contribute steadily to tribal welfare and prosperity, especially considering their population in the region and the fact that the majority of them live in the interior parts of the forests. It is important to continue to support PFM initiatives in the region and to ensure the welfare of tribal communities in the long run.

A Glimpse of Community Services Provided in North Wayanad through PFM.

Chapter – 16

Vanaamritham in Mannarkad

The Vanaamritham project is a community-based initiative that is empowering tribal communities in the Attapady region aimed at improving their livelihoods and conservation of forests. The project is being implemented by the Mannarkad FDA in collaboration with various Vana Samarkshana Samiths (VSS). The tribal communities of Kadukmanna, Dhanyam, Pettikkal, Sambarcode, Melechavadiyoor, and Moolakombu (in the region) collect a variety of forest products, including sticky desmodium (moovila), country mallow (kurunthotti), turkey berry plant (chunda), thippli (indian long pepper), indian sarsaparilla (nannari), pata root (pada veru), honey, dammar, and ottila.

The collection of NTFPs, processing, and sales remain the most important occupation of the tribal communities in the Attappadi region. However, they have been facing exploitation by middlemen for years. To address this issue, the Vanamritham project was launched by the Mannardkad FDA. The project aims to consolidate the collection of NTFPs through VSS and to sell them directly to Ayurveda companies. This eliminates the middlemen who have traditionally exploited tribal communities by paying them low prices for their produce. The main features of the project are as follows:

- Implementation through PFM institutions (VSS): The project is being implemented through PFM institutions (VSS) in the Attappady region.
- Participation of Kurumba Irula and Muduka tribal groups: These tribal communities in the Attapadi region are participants in the project.
- Higher prices for NTFPs: Such forest resources fetch higher prices than prevailing prices at the time of transfer of produce from the tribal communities to Ayurvedic companies.

- Direct supply to Ayurveda companies: Supply of NTFPs directly to Ayurvedic companies by eliminating the use of middlemen.

- Unadulterated herbs for Ayurvedic companies: Unadulterated herbs are made available to Ayurvedic companies.

- Regular inspection and evaluation: The activities of the project are inspected and evaluated at every stage under the supervision of Mannarkkad FDA.

- Job opportunities for tribal groups: Tribal communities have been able to enjoy many job opportunities in this sector.

- New source of revenue for government: The FDA has created a new source of revenue in the form of GST.

- Higher value through tendering: Due to the tendering process, higher value is obtained for such products and the profit from the marketing of such products also accrues to the tribal communities.

- Cultivation of plants required by Ayurvedic companies: Steps are also being taken at the FDA level to initiate the cultivation of plants required by such Ayurvedic companies in the next phase of the project.

In the next phase, more communities will be included in the scheme. Steps are being taken to expand the scheme as well.

The Vanaamritham project helps tribal communities to sell NTFPs in a well-organized manner, through PFM institutions and the FDA. This helps to ensure that they get a fair price for their produce, and generate stable employment opportunities. VSS provides tribal communities with regular employment opportunities and helps them to develop their skills in the collection and processing of NTFPs and ensure high-quality raw materials for the production of Ayurveda medicines. The FDA works with Ayurveda companies to ensure that the NTFPs they collect are of the highest quality.

This project is a successful example of how community-based initiatives can be used to improve the livelihoods of tribal communities and conserve forests. The project is also providing valuable insights into how to develop sustainable models for the collection and utilization of NTFPs. In addition to the economic benefits, the Vanaamritham project is also having a positive impact on the social and cultural well-being of tribal communities in the Attapady region.

The project is helping to empower tribal communities and give them a greater voice in the management of their forests and other natural resources. This project is a valuable model for other communities that are working to improve their livelihoods and conserve their forests. The project has demonstrated that it is possible to strike a balance between economic development and environmental conservation.

Tribal Communities in Mannarkad are Actively Participating in the Vanaamritham Project.

Chapter – 17

The Efforts in Punalur Forest Division

Punalur, also called the City of Water, is a famous town in the eastern part of the Kollam district in Kerala. It is located on the banks of the Kallada River and borders Tamil Nadu. Punalur is famous for many things, including its historic hanging bridge and scenic beauty.

Punalur FDA is striving to create alternative sources of livelihood for forest-dependent communities by providing financial and other types of logistic support. To help VSS members generate income, Punalur FDA has provided Rs 40,000 as a grant. With this money, VSS members have started a variety of income-generation ventures.

Income Generation Projects

The Cherukdavu VSS members have formed a women's Slef-help Group (SHG) that manufactures and sells *wrightia tinctoria* (danthapala) oil, handmade aloe vera soap, and cleaning lotion. All three products, especially the handmade aloe vera soap, are in high demand. The SHG members sell their products locally and have created a space in the highly competitive market. They are in the process of mechanizing the soap production unit. This benefits 10 women members and their families.

The FDA has helped to constitute mushroom cultivation through 20 SHGs by providing training and other necessary logistics. They are also given support to market the products locally. Yet another initiative is the creation of bee nests. The FDA has distributed 20 bee nests to seven VSS each. The honey produced will be marketed and sold under a separate brand as 'Nattuthen'. The idea is to produce high-quality organic honey. This is expected to encourage sustainable honey bee farming and will also reduce the dependency on forest honey. Over 120 VSS members will benefit from the project. The VSS members in Punalur have also ventured into bamboo craft, spice powder production, cultivation of medicinal plants, and manufacturing cloth bags. Driven by the admiration for their craftsmanship, VSS members have begun exporting their exquisite handicrafts.

Revival of 'Kaalattam' - A Unique Art Form of Kani Tribal Community

Kaalattam is a unique art form practiced by the Kani tribe living in the Kadamancode and Kocharippara areas of Punalur. It is a mixture of dance and music, backed by certain instruments. The Kani tribe has been practicing it as part of their traditional art forms for generations. They perform the Kaalattam in temples and other important functions.

In recent years, the art form has been on the verge of dying out. However, the Punalur FDA has intervened and given it hope for revival by professionalizing the art form. The FDA is also working to promote Kaalattam to tourists and other visitors to the Punalur area to help them identify potential stages elsewhere. The effort taken to revive Kaalattam is a testament to the resilience of the Kani tribe and their commitment to preserving their traditional culture. It is also a reminder of the importance of the Forest Department in supporting indigenous art forms, through PFM.

As part of efforts to revitalize the Kaalattam art form, a public display was held at the Koyikkal Palace in Thiruvananthapuram, hosted by the Kerala State Department of Archaeology in 2023. The event was met with rave reviews.

VSS Members in Punalur FDA Creating Exquisite Handicrafts.

Chapter – 18
Climate Resilience Efforts and PFM

Climate change, which is causing concern around the world, has also affected Kerala (Hunt & Menon, 2020). Flash floods, unexpected heavy rains, wildfires, sea level rise, and landslides are all major warnings for Kerala. In this situation, the Kerala government has released the "Environment Restoration Policy 2021" aimed at ensuring environmental security. This policy framework envisages comprehensive action plans that give priority to the restoration of forests and other ecosystems, including the avoidance of monoculture plantations such as acacia and eucalyptus, the removal of invasive plant-animal guilds, soil, and water conservation activities, and the protection of wetlands.

Environment restoration activities are very much required for the forests that are losing biodiversity and are on the verge of destruction. Such activities are being implemented with the participation of forest-dependent communities through PFM institutions. Such model activities improve environmental security and water security, while also creating employment opportunities for forest-dependent people. A couple of successful models are discussed below.

Harithavasantham EDC: A Model of Community-Based Environmental Restoration

Harithavasantham EDC in the Munnar Wildlife (Anamudi) Division is a shining example of a people's collective that has made significant strides in environmental restoration. Through the active participation of local communities, Harithavasantham EDC members have successfully restored grasslands, small streams, and streams in Vattavada, bringing back not only the biodiversity but also the overall vegetation in the region.

101

Aanapantham VSS: Restoring - Failed Teak Plantations

The Aanapantham VSS, a forest-dependent tribal community in the Chalakudy Forest Division, has demonstrated the remarkable power of community-based conservation. With their deep understanding of the local ecosystem, they have successfully transformed a failed 10-hectare teak plantation back into natural forests. Their efforts have not only revived the plantation but also enriched the biodiversity of the area.

Pillapara AVSS: Encountering Soil Erosion

In response to the growing threat of soil erosion caused by severe floods, the members of the Pillapara AVSS have undertaken a commendable initiative to plant tree saplings along the banks of the Chalakudy River. To date, they have successfully planted 8,000 indigenous saplings of five resilient and beneficial tree species: *aegle marmelos (bael), garcinia gummi-gutta, bambusa bamboo, terminalia arjuna (arjuna), and mimusops elengi (spanish plum)*. This has also contributed to the restoration of the natural habitat in the area.

North Wayanad Forest Division: Harnessing Tribal Knowledge for Invasive Plant Removal

The North Wayanad FDA has recognized the invaluable traditional knowledge and expertise of tribal communities like the Kaatunaika and Adiya in tackling the issue of invasive plants. By collaborating with these communities, through Plamoola VSS the FDA has effectively engaged in removing invasive plants from the forest, restoring its natural balance and resilience. The North Wayanad Forest Division has taken a bold step in reclaiming land from invasive species. Through their dedicated efforts, they have successfully removed invasive plants like *West Indian Lantana* (Aripoo) and *Chromolaena Odorata* (Communist Green) from a 20-hectare forest area, restoring it to its natural state. Their work serves as a testament to the power of collective action in environmental restoration.

Muttanga, Ponkuzhi, Puthur, Kattampakad, and Punchi EDC: Turning Invasive Plants into Sustainable Products

In an innovative approach to utilizing invasive plants, the members of Muttanga, Ponkuzhi, Puthur, Kattampakad, and Punchi EDC in the Wayanad Wildlife Sanctuary have transformed the invasive *West Indian Lantana* plant into a source of livelihood. By manufacturing decorative items and wooden products from this once-problematic plant, the members of these EDC have demonstrated the potential to convert environmental challenges into sustainable opportunities.

Chollanavayal VSS – Guardians of Nature

Forest-dependent communities are well-recognized for their deep connection to and commitment to sustainable forest conservation. This strong sense of ownership fosters a strong determination to protect their forests, as evidenced by a recent incident in Ranni. The members of Chollanavayal VSS have taken it upon themselves to guard the multipurpose miscellaneous hardwood species plantations in the Karikkulam-Moongappara forest. This commendable initiative safeguards over 16,000 tree saplings, including fruit-bearing jackfruit and wild jack, which will ultimately contribute to retaining wildlife within the forest. Their watch over the plantation is continuous, spanning day and night

These remarkable examples highlight the transformative power of community-based environmental restoration. By harnessing the knowledge, skills, and dedication of local communities, it is possible to effectively restore degraded ecosystems, protect biodiversity, and create sustainable livelihoods. The stories of Harithavasantham EDC, Aanapantham VSS, the North Wayanad Forest Division, and the Wayanad Wildlife

Sanctuary EDC serve as beacons of hope, inspiring everyone to embrace community-driven participatory approaches to environmental and forest conservation.

In the last two years, PFM activities have resulted in increasing the extent of forest area in Kerala to 823 square kilometers which is due to the execution of participatory approaches in forest conservation. At the same time, the carbon storage of forests in Kerala also increased to 21.29 million tons.

The unwavering commitment of the forest-dependent communities has been instrumental in safeguarding Kerala's forests from the threat of wildfires. These dedicated individuals serve as the frontline defenders of our precious forest ecosystems, playing a crucial role in preventing and extinguishing forest fires. Their timely interventions have averted countless disasters, protecting not only the forests but also the lives and livelihoods of countless people who depend on them.

Chapter – 19

Forest Rights Act and PFM

The Forest Rights Act (FRA) of 2006 is one of the most debated and discussed aspects of forestry in India today (Münster & Vishnudas, 2012). It is considered a significant piece of legislation that recognizes the rights of tribal communities and other traditional forest dwellers to the forest resources on which they depend for their livelihood and cultural needs. The Act also emphasizes the protection of forests and wildlife and empowers Gram Sabhas to have a decisive say in the determination of local policies and schemes impacting them (Mohanty, 2015).

The FRA encompasses three important rights: Individual rights, Community rights, and Developmental rights. Individual rights include the right to self-cultivation and habitation, the right to grazing, fishing, and access to water bodies in forests, and the right to protect, regenerate, conserve, or manage community forest resources for sustainable use. Community rights include the right to habitat for Particularly Vulnerable Tribal Groups (PVTGs), the right to traditional seasonal resource access for nomadic and pastoral communities, the right to access to biodiversity, the community right to intellectual property and traditional knowledge, and the recognition of traditional customary rights. Developmental rights ensure the allocation of forest land for developmental purposes by fulfilling the basic infrastructural requirements of the community.

PFM on the other hand, aims at the sustainable management of forests, creating alternative livelihoods, and empowering forest-dependent communities (Perera, 2009),(Kjosavik, & Shanmugaratnam, 2021). There are distinct differences between the FRA and PFM approaches. FRA stands as a legally binding statute that grants forest rights to individuals and communities, while PFM is a more voluntary approach based on government orders. FRA prioritizes recognizing and safeguarding the rights of forest-dependent communities. Conversely, PFM focuses on promoting sustainable forest management practices.

Some potential tensions have emerged between these approaches. A few staunch FRA advocates have severely criticized PFM. Organizations like the Campaign for Survival and Dignity (an Indian national forum for tribal and forest dwellers) consider PFM illegal, hazardous, and an instrument of the Forest Department. However, blind criticism of PFM as a scam by such groups is tasteless by all means. Even if PFM has had shortcomings, it has played a vital role in empowering forest-dependent communities. Most of these shortcomings have arisen from bureaucratic mishaps, not from the PFM approach itself.

The Forest Department should be considered an important agency involved in implementing the FRA. In Kerala, "Tribal welfare" is an integral part of the PFM programs managed by the Eco-development and Tribal Welfare Wing through the State Forest Development Agency (SFDA) and Forest Development Agencies (FDAs) of the Kerala Forests Department. In reality, the Forest Department plays a vital role in implementing the FRA without compromising its objective of protection and conservation of forest resources, although the Act proposes a marginal role for the department.

It is noteworthy that the rights mentioned in the Forest Rights Act, such as the right to own NTFPs within and outside village boundaries, the right to access and collect fish and other products from waterbodies, the right to community tenures of habitat and habitation for particularly vulnerable tribal groups (PVTGs), the right to protect, regenerate, conserve, or manage any community forest resource that has been traditionally protected and conserved for sustainable use, and the right to access biodiversity and traditional knowledge related to biodiversity and cultural diversity, are already being exercised by forest-dependent communities through PFM institutions since they ensure the preservation of the habitat of forest-dwelling scheduled tribes from any forms of destructive practices that affect their cultural and natural heritage.

Despite its shortcomings, criticisms, and pitfalls, the Forest Department has played a crucial role in preserving and conserving forest cover as well as empowering forest-dependent communities through PFM over the years. However, it seems that the advocates of the FRA are trying their best to undermine the historic role of Forest Departments in India.

The role of the Forest Department in the successful implementation of FRA and its role in protecting forests cannot be belittled or dismissed in the guise of FRA implementation. The Forest Department will continue to move forward and fulfill its mandate of forest protection.

PFM-FRA Convergence

The FRA is a continuation and progression of the National Forest Conservation Policy of 1988, which led to the evolution of PFM in Kerala in the mid-1990s. Over the years, the forest department has ensured the rights of scheduled tribes through the successful implementation of various participatory programs through PFM institutions. The community rights and duty provisions have already been implemented through PFM by the forest department. The proposed community rights can be seen as the major connecting link between PFM and FRA implementation. The forest department should take on more responsibility and have an equal role with the tribal development department in implementing the FRA.

FRA can be used to identify and map traditional forest rights, which can be incorporated into PFM microplans. PFM can help communities exercise their FRA rights by providing support with claiming and documenting their rights. FRA can provide a legal basis for PFM agreements, which can help ensure that these agreements are enforceable and accountable. PFM can be used to implement FRA's provisions on community forest management, which can help ensure that these provisions are implemented effectively and sustainably.

Both Participatory Forest Management (PFM) and the Forest Rights Act (FRA) are complementary strategies for sustainable forest conservation and the empowerment of forest-dependent communities in India. These approaches should be given adequate space to build a well-balanced and comprehensive future for forest-dependent communities. They should be utilized to create a just and equitable system of forest governance in India, one that empowers local communities to manage their forests sustainably for the benefit of all.

Chapter – 20

PFM in the Age of Post-Modernity, Artificial Intelligence & Technological Advancements

At least some may tend to consider that an approach like PFM doesn't have much worth in the age of postmodernity, artificial intelligence, and space technology. However, on the contrary, it has immense value in sustaining human lives, since 'forests and humans have a common future'. Postmodernity has challenged the traditional notion of knowledge and authority, and it has emphasized the importance of local perspectives and participation. This is in line with the principles of PFM that provide local communities a democratic space, and voice in the management of their forests. PFM as a democratic community approach is a relief from the traditional hierarchical system of the State as it echoes the rights of the forest dwellers by providing more voice through a democratic and decentralized platform. However, PFM does not challenge the traditional knowledge of the forest-dependent communities, rather it fosters such knowledge for the overall benefit of forest dwellers and the sustainable conservation of forest resources. It is also in line with populism which emphasizes the idea of "the people", and claims to champion the common person. PFM asserts to champion sustainable forest conservation through "forest-dependent communities" that are often marginalized in society. In PFM, populism is not used in political terms, rather it is about giving a stake and voice to the forest-dependent communities, i.e. giving voice to the masses.

Human society is undergoing a rapid and continuous revolution, with advancements like Artificial Intelligence (AI) and other cutting-edge technologies. These changes can be harnessed to significantly improve PFM and the welfare of forest-dependent communities. Mobile applications, drones, and other technologies can be employed for various PFM tasks, including preparing micro plans, assessing

NTFPs, collecting data on forest resources, professionalizing NTFP collection and management, and combating forest fires. Additionally, providing online training and capacity building for forest officials and forest-dependent communities can reduce costs and save time. Developing mobile apps with basic information about forests, forest maps, and forest resources can facilitate communication, streamline data collection, and empower communities to actively participate in forest management activities.

It is not wise to resist Artificial intelligence (AI) or any such technological advancements but make optimum and judicious use of it for the betterment of participatory approach and conservation of forest resources. AI can be used to analyze satellite imagery to detect deforestation and other forest disturbances. It can also be used to develop models of forest growth and dynamics, which can help forest officials make better decisions about how to manage forests. It can also be used to assist in office operations to prepare projects thereby saving time and costs. Space technology can also be used to develop communication and information systems that can help connect forest communities with government agencies and other stakeholders. For example, satellite imagery can be used to monitor forest cover and to track the movement of illegal logging operations.

PFM will continue to move forward despite technological advancements and scientific inventions since such inventions can only be used to enhance participatory forest management and not to replace it. Its contribution to sustaining forest resources, fighting climate change, and enhancing the lives of forest-dependent communities will continue to grow.

Epilogue

To gain a comprehensive understanding of PFM, it is it's crucial to analyze its successes while critically evaluating its shortcomings. There is a famous saying "Bureaucracy has its lag". As the saying, the complexities and delays in bureaucracy have in many ways affected the progress of PFM in Kerala. Mostly enormous efforts are required to overcome 'red-tapism' and problems of bureaucracy. Forest officials are also bound with a considerable number of forest protection duties and responsibilities. Hence, many of them find it challenging to cater to PFM. The success of many of the PFM institutions has not yet been replicated all over the State. Many projects initiated by PFM institutions have not yielded the expected results due to lack of follow-up, and mishaps in implementation.

It equally takes a massive effort to generate interest in a particular project among forest-dependent communities. Rigorous and continuous monitoring of the projects undertaken by the tribal communities is required from the part of the forest officials to ensure success. Hence, success and failure depend upon the interest, and efforts taken by the responsible forest officers since a lot of energy is to be invested in sustaining the income generation initiatives. At least some officials have envisaged PFM as a threat to their authority over forest management and forest-dependent communities which has resulted in delays in the execution of participatory programs and projects. They also tend to apply rigorous bureaucratic control on PFM which ultimately questions the freedom of operation. The question of responsibility also applies to both officials and forest-dependent communities. Hence more caution and responsibility are to be exercised in using their authority to protect forest resources. On the other hand, at least some forest-dependent communities tend to consider PFM as only a tool to reap social and economic benefits over anything else. A fair balance is to be practiced between bureaucracy and forest dwellers. External forces like political parties also tend to influence PFM institutions. In several cases, such political interferences have halted the functioning and the progress made by these grassroots-level institutions.

Regardless of the ongoing interventions, welfare programs, and projects, much effort is required for the total and comprehensive upliftment of the tribal communities who are facing a considerable number of challenges (alcoholism, poverty, health and hygiene, infant mortality, and various other problems) in a post-modern world.

Another challenge is ensuring appropriate representation of forest-dependent communities in decision-making processes. This is important because these communities have a vested interest in the sustainable management of forest resources. Another task is to ensure that PFM programs are adequately funded. However, money alone will not be enough, because the actual success of projects and programs depends on the effective utilization of funds. In several cases, funds get mismanaged or underutilized due to the varying interests of forest officials responsible for such purposes. Lack of continuous training and follow-ups have also adversely affected the progress of PFM in the state. Another factor hindering PFM's progress is the lack of communication between offices at the Forest Circles and Divisions. Delays in responding to various requirements by Circle and Division offices significantly impede PFM's progress. Furthermore, their inadequate understanding of PFM principles and practices poses an additional challenge that needs to be addressed.

It is a well-known fact that PFM has never been the priority for many forest officials, which has proved to be yet another difficulty. Moreover, the social nature of PFM has always remained a herculean task for several traditional forest officers. They find it hard to strike a balance between PFM and forest protection, despite the strong interlinkage between the two. There has been a tendency on the part of at least some officials to prioritize quantitative programs like infrastructure development and income generation, while qualitative aspects like outreach programs and support services are given the least priority. However, this is not the case always.

Framing policies for PFM is an area that requires a lot of rethinking and rigorous exercise, along with timely updates, the formation of policies based on changing needs, and the scope for social audits of projects and welfare programs. These aspects are to be formulated based on the changing ground realities rather than from the point of view of bureaucracy alone. Considering the enormous human and other resources involved in PFM, there exist huge opportunities to excel in diverse manners. However, the absence of visionary and far-fetched programs and projects has resulted in halting the progress of PFM to a greater extent, and the huge potential of the human resources involved remains underutilized.

The postmodern worldview emphasizes self-expression rather than deference to authority. Participation and self-expression of forest-dependent communities are crucial to the success of PFM. However, the question of authentic participation and the extent of their stake in decision-making remains a concern. In many instances, the interests and needs of participating communities and realities in the field may not be effectively conveyed to the top hierarchy of the Forest Department. The department's flow of authority remains top-down, and execution officers such as range forest officers, deputy rangers, beat forest officers, and section forest officers play a critical role in balancing relations between the top forest hierarchy (policy framers and decision-makers) and forest-dependent communities. They are also responsible for implementing PFM policies and programs at the grassroots level, and their actions have a direct impact on the relationship between forest-dependent communities and the Forest Department. Unfortunately, instances of manipulation, corruption, bribery, and abuse of power are not uncommon. Despite these challenges, grassroots-level PFM institutions have emerged to challenge such authority to some extent. However, in bureaucratic settings, the hierarchy is not always inclined to heed such challenges, even in the 21st century, particularly in a country like India. Bureaucratic structures can

114

often drown out the voices of forest-dependent communities during decision-making, leading to the systematic undercutting of their needs and perspectives.

The feudalistic mentality of some bureaucrats, the influence of political parties on PFM institutions, and delays in governmental procedures can hinder the effectiveness of PFM initiatives and prevent them from achieving the expected results. Such mentality may also result in a reluctance to delegate authority to local communities, a lack of transparency in decision-making processes, and a resistance to change which results in obstacles to genuine participation by communities, which is essential for the success of PFM.

Another persistent issue is the vilification of the Forest Department. Some segments of society tend to blame the Forest Department as the primary cause of problems faced by tribal communities and issues with sustainable forest management and conservation. Since FRA is being touted as the ultimate solution to the problems of tribal communities, its supporters have made every effort to undermine the role of the Forest Department in every aspect. This has further eroded the department's image in several ways.

Political interference can also pose significant challenges to PFM. Political parties may attempt to influence PFM decisions for their benefit, rather than considering the long-term interests of the forests and the communities that depend on them. This can lead to unsustainable practices, corruption, and a lack of accountability.

The drastic changes in the socio-political and economic landscape, including those impacting forest-dependent communities (particularly tribal communities' lifestyles), climate and environmental challenges, and evolving state forest management policies, all necessitate prioritizing the strengthening of PFM institutions. However, a crucial question remains: are these democratic institutions being strengthened most effectively? Mental health-related problems and substance abuse are major areas of concern for tribal communities. Additionally, their changing food habits (switching from organic to modern, processed, and potentially adulterated food) have resulted in significant health issues. However, it remains uncertain whether PFM institutions are being fully utilized as a democratic platform to address these challenges.

Another pressing problem is the recent Forest (Conservation) Amendment Act, 2023 (FCAA) which amends the Forest (Conservation) Act, of 1980. The Forest (Conservation) Amendment Bill 2023 was passed by the Lok Sabha on July 26, 2023. This Bill makes it easier to build roads and other construction projects near borders without needing permission to cut down trees. The problem is that this could lead to cutting down forests in ecologically sensitive areas, especially in the mountains and near borders. Another problem is that the law only considers land officially listed as a forest to be protected. This could hurt the rights of tribal communities who live in forested areas but the land isn't officially listed. Many are worried that this law will damage the environment, harm tribal communities, and question their rights. The Forest Rights Act (FRA) stands as a shield for tribal communities' forest rights. However, recent amendments and bills, like the Forest (Conservation) Amendment Act of 2023, threaten those same rights. This complex situation demands clear solutions and also highlights the immense potential of strengthened PFM institutions. Given these growing challenges, PFM institutions hold immense potential. Empowering forest-dependent communities by strengthening PFM institutions becomes crucial. However, both the FRA and the Forest (Conservation) Amendment Bill fall under the government's purview. Unfortunately, the Forest Department, being a government agency, faces limitations due to its bureaucratic nature.

Regardless of its two-and-a-half decades of existence, PFM has not gained widespread public attention in the State. It remains a topic of limited discussion and debate in the public sphere. The Forest Department is frequently the subject of discussions and debates in print and visual media, however, PFM, its human face remains largely hidden from view. While PFM activities do receive some media coverage, the attention given to this important initiative is not adequate for its significance and impact on the lives of forest-dependent communities.

Born in the same era, Kerala's decentralization has soared while PFM stumbles, despite substantial investment. This disparity raises questions about the effectiveness of PFM models in the state. While Kerala boasts a shining example of decentralization, its PFM story is one of persistent struggle. The state's success in one sphere throws into stark relief the challenges facing the other, demanding a deeper examination of strategies and implementation. PFM's struggles call for a renewed focus on community participation, innovative strategies, and a re-evaluation of existing frameworks to ensure both initiatives contribute to sustainable forest management and empowered communities.

The Quest for Improvement

Advancing PFM hinges on a paradigm shift in the mindset and practices of forest bureaucrats, coupled with substantive systemic reforms. Such transformations cannot be achieved overnight. The entrenched rigidity of India's bureaucratic apparatus demands unwavering dedication and passion from forest officials, from the clerical level to the highest echelons of the department. While crafting supportive policies, projects, acts, and laws favouring forest-dependent communities and participatory approaches is crucial, their effectiveness ultimately depends on their implementation at the grassroots level.

The protection and sustainable conservation of forests stand as paramount responsibilities for forest officials. However, achieving this objective demands a combination of these fundamental principles with a practical and thorough understanding of ground realities. To enhance the efficacy of PFM, several measures can be implemented, including the judicious allocation of funds, rigorous social audits, adherence to ethical practices, fostering accountability, promoting transparent decision-making, and demonstrating social commitment. Regular training and follow-ups, coupled with the engagement of academic institutions, researchers, NGOs, professionals, and activists, engaging with tribal and forest-dependent communities in all aspects of forest management, enhancing participatory approach, addressing the underlying causes of deforestation and forest degradation and intensifying the engagement of tribal and forest-dependent through PFM institutions to compact such issues are some of the crucial steps towards developing a comprehensive approach for the overall improvement of PFM.

PFM - Pedagogy of Tribal, Indigenous, and Traditional Forest-Dependent Communities

As Paulo Freire states in his landmark work 'Pedagogy of the Oppressed' that dialogue is an act of "love, humility, and faith" in humanity. It also requires hope, mutual trust, and critical thinking from the people who are in dialogue together. Dialogue consists of both thoughts and concrete actions together. Freire's central thesis is that education can be a tool for liberation, or it can be a tool for oppression. He argues that the traditional model of education, in which teachers deposit knowledge into students' heads, is oppressive because it teaches students to passively accept the world as it is. Instead, Freire advocates for a "problem-posing" model of education, in which teachers and students work together to analyze and solve real-world problems.

Likewise, PFM is an approach that challenges the traditional policing system of forest conservation thereby alienating the forest-dependent communities from the State. Instead, it encourages forest officials to engage in discourse with the forest-dependent communities and to find amicable solutions to their problems. PFM is not limited to discourses and interactions, rather it guarantees the formation of basic grassroots-level democratic institutions through which various community-oriented projects and programs are executed at their best. Even though PFM institutions operate by the guidelines mandated by the Forest Department, they enjoy enormous liberty in operation.

Despite the challenges and shortcomings, PFM is often referred to as the 'human face' of the Forest Department in Kerala because of its collaborative approach to forest management that involves the participation of forest-dependent communities. It is one of the most innovative, democratic, and decentralized approaches in the history of forest management in the State. PFM has played a key role in strengthening the relationship between the forest-dependent communities and the forest department. In the past, the Forest Department was often seen as an intimidating force, responsible for enforcing forest laws and regulations. This led to a sense of alienation and distrust among forest-dependent communities. However, the sharing and caring approach through PFM has helped to bridge this gap by giving communities a space for their voice to be heard in the management and conservation of forests. PFM has heralded a groundbreaking shift in the relationship between forest-dependent communities and forest officials, ushering in an era of shared decision-making and democratization. It is a fact that over the past two and a half decades, PFM has played a vital role in shifting the approach towards forest conservation in Kerala i.e. from a traditional policing method to a people-oriented system. PFM has revolutionized the role of people (tribal and forest-dependent communities) in forest management. It is a promising approach to forest management that has the potential to achieve multiple benefits.

PFM has contributed to social awakening for the Forest Department and forest-dependent communities alike. Social awakening is a process by which people become aware of their social and political rights and responsibilities. Both parties have recognized the growing need for sustainable forest conservation. PFM has facilitated the Forest Department's outreach to forest-dependent communities and engagement in implementing welfare and empowerment programs. PFM has also fostered community cohesion by bringing people together for a common goal, promoting cooperation, and fostering mutual understanding. Over the years, it has reinforced the values of democracy in resource management. It has motivated forest-dependent communities to take ownership of their resources. PFM has contributed to the creation of social capital by strengthening relationships among forest-dependent communities, the Forest Department, and the forests themselves, fostering trust and cooperation. It has also played a significant role in peace and reconciliation efforts.

PFM is not limited to the implementation of certain income-generation projects. Rather, it has enabled the forest authorities in the state to reach out to all stakeholders of forest conservation, including local communities, NGOs, and government agencies. This has helped to create a more collaborative approach to sustainable forest management. In addition to alternative income generation, PFM has contributed to building relationships and creating a sense of shared ownership of forest resources. Despite its shortcomings, PFM has fostered a long-lasting fellowship between the state mechanism and the forest-dependent communities. It has also resulted in creating a lasting impact on the lives of forest-dependent communities.

About the Authors

George Alexander

George Alexander is a writer, orator, and trainer with over 13 years of experience in human resources and management. He has worked in diverse corporate, government, academic, and non-profit environments. He holds two master's degrees, one in social work with specialization in urban and rural community development and the other in philosophy with specialization in social transformation and empowerment. He is a board member of the Occidental Studies Institute (OSI) and has published 10 books and numerous articles.

Email: georgy1234@gmail.com

Lijo P George

Lijo P. George is a social scientist and ethnographer with a diverse range of research interests in sociology, anthropology, rural development, and tribal studies. He holds a Ph.D. in sociology from the University of Kerala and has published numerous articles in esteemed journals on tribal sociology, environmental studies, forest sociology, human-animal conflicts, climate resilience, and society, etc.

Email: lijogeorge101@gmail.com

References:

1. Ahenkan, A., & Boon, E. (2011). Non-timber forest products (NTFPs): Clearing the confusion in semantics. *Journal of Human Ecology*, *33*(1), 1-9.

2. Ajin,V.C.(2022). Vanasree- Vanasritharuda Mughasree (Malayalam). Forestry Information Bureau. Government of Kerala. *Aranyam Magazine* 41 (11-12).

3. Alex, A., & Vidyasagaran, K. (2016). The marketing of non-timber forest products in the Western Ghats region of Attappady, Kerala. *Economic Affairs*, *61*(3), 355-363.

4. Alexander, George (2021).Mattathinte Mathrikyayi Mancode (Malayalam). Forestry Information Bureau. Government of Kerala, *Aranyam Magazine*. 41 (11- 12).

5. Alexander,George(2022).Vanam-Vaaakuppum-eco-tourisavum (Malayalam). Forestry Information Bureau. Government of Kerala. *Aranyam Magazine* 42 (12).

6. Arun, L. K., Jayasankar, B., & Abraham, K. M. (2001). *Biodiversity conservation and livelihood issues of tribe's folk: A case study of Periyar Tiger Reserve* (No. 37). Centre for Development Studies.

7. Augustine, R. (2022). Tribal population and skill development programme a study of Idukki district in Kerala. Doctoral dissertation, Christ University.

8. Bengtsson, J., Bullock, J. M., Egoh, B., Everson, C., Everson, T., O'connor, T., & Lindborg, R. (2019). Grasslands—more important for ecosystem services than you might think. *Ecosphere*, *10*(2).

9. Bhardwaj, A., Bhardwaj, A. K., Vinod, T. R., Anoop, K. R., Sunil, C. G., Ram, V. M.,& Mathew, J. (2023). Redefining conservation: eco-development initiatives in Periyar Tiger Reserve, India. *Journeys to more equitable and effective*

conservation: the central role of Indigenous peoples and local communities. Iucn Commission On Environmental, Economic And Social Policy, 23 (23).

10. Bhattacharya, P., Pradhan, L., & Yadav, G. (2010). Joint forest management in India: experiences of two decades. Resources, Conservation and Recycling, 54(8), 469-480.

11. Bisui, S., Roy, S., Bera, B., Adhikary, P. P., Sengupta, D., Bhunia, G. S., & Shit, P. K. (2023). Economical and ecological realization of Joint Forest Management (JFM) for sustainable rural livelihood: a case study. *Tropical Ecology*, 64(2), 296-306.

12. Census (2011). District Census Handbook, Registrar General of India, Ministry of Home Affairs and Government of India. Available at: http://www.censusindia.gov.

13. Chandran, C., & Bhattacharya, P. (2021). Perception of visitors on ecotourism environmental impact: A study of Munnar, Kerala, India. *World Journal of Environmental Biosciences*, *10*(2), 1-8.

14. Chundamannil.(1983). History of Forest Management in Kerala. KFRI Research Report.

15. Damayanti, E. K., & Masuda, M. (2008). Implementation process of India Ecodevelopment Project and the sustainability: Lessons from Periyar Tiger Reserve in Kerala State, India. *Tropics*, *17*(2), 147-158.

16. Das, M., & Chatterjee, B. (2015). Ecotourism: A panacea or a predicament?. *Tourism management perspectives*, *14*, 3-16.

17. Das, V. (1996). Minor Forest Produce and Rights of Tribals. Economic and Political Weekly, 3227-3229.

18. Devi, P., & Suresh Kumar, P. (2012). Traditional, ethnic, and fermented foods of different tribes of Manipur. *Indian Journal of Traditional Knowledge* Vol. 11(1), January 2012, pp. 70-77

19. Devika, J. (2016). Participatory democracy or 'transformative appropriation'? The people's planning campaign in Kerala. *History and Sociology of South Asia, 10*(2), 115-137.

20. Dhali, M. K. (2015). Socio-Economic Status in a Hilly Region: A Case Study of Munnar, Idukki District, Kerala, India. *International research journal of social sciences, 4*(12), 1-6.

21. Dhanapal, G. (2019). Revisiting participatory forest management in India. *Current Science,* 117(7), 1161-1166.

22. Edward, M., & George, B. (2008). Tourism development in the state of Kerala, India: A study of destination attractiveness. *European journal of tourism research, 1*(1), 16-38.

23. Edward, M., & Kumar, R. R. (2017). Ecotourism in Kerala-a case study on empowering the indigenous community. *International Journal of Qualitative Research in Services,* 2(4), 295-307.

24. Egoh, B. N., Bengtsson, J., Lindborg, R., Bullock, J. M., Dixon, A. P., & Rouget, M. (2016). The importance of grasslands in providing ecosystem services: opportunities for poverty alleviation. In *Routledge handbook of ecosystem services* (pp. 421-441). Routledge.

25. Fennell, D. A. (2013). Ecotourism and ethics. R. *Ballantyne & J. Packer, International Handbook on Ecotourism,* 31-42.

26. Fennell, D. A. (2014). Ecotourism. Routledge.

27. Gaujour, E., Amiaud, B., Mignolet, C., & Plantureux, S. (2012). Factors and processes affecting plant biodiversity in permanent grasslands. A review. *Agronomy for sustainable development, 32*(1), 133-160.

28. Geiser, U. (2001). To 'participate with whom, for what (and against whom): forest fringe management along the Western Ghats in southern Kerala. In

Analytical Issues in Participatory Natural Resource Management, London: Palgrave Macmillan UK (pp. 19-36).

29. Geiser, U. (2017). Reading 'participation in forest management' through 'modern' and 'post-modern' concepts, or: where to start normative debates? In Food, Nature and Society (pp. 209-231). Routledge.

30. George M, Veena & G., Christopher. (2017). Nutritional value of selected wild edible leaves used by tribal communities of Attappady, Southern Western Ghats. 2. 2455-4898.

31. George, S. (2018). Migration and social history of Anjunadu: Lessons from the past for sustainable development–An applied study. PESQUISA, 3(2).

32. Gopakumar, C. S., Prasada Rao, G. S. L. H. V., & Ram Mohan, H. S. (2011). *Impacts of climate variability on agriculture in Kerala* (Doctoral dissertation, Cochin University of Science & Technology).

33. Gopinath, P. P., Nishan, M. A., Durga, A. R., Gopakumar, S., Lazarus, T. P., & Jerin, V. A. (2022). Role of Non-Timber Forest Products in Income Generation of the Tribal Population: A Review. *Asian Journal of Agricultural Extension, Economics & Sociology, 40*(11), 285-294.

34. Gowri, M. U., & Shivakumar, K. M. (2020). Millet scenario in India. Economic Affairs, 65(3), 363-370.

35. Guha, A., Pradhan, A., & Mondal, K. (2000). Joint forest management in West Bengal: a long way to go. *Journal of Human Ecology, 11*(6), 471-476.

36. Gurukkal, R. (2003). The eco-development project and the socioeconomics of the fringe area of the Periyar Tiger Reserve: a concurrent study. *Report, School of Social Sciences, Mahatma Gandhi University, Kottayam, India.*

37. Hunt, K. M., & Menon, A. (2020). The 2018 Kerala floods: a climate change perspective. *Climate Dynamics, 54*(3-4), 2433-2446.

38. Isac, S. (2011). Education and socio-cultural reproduction: Development of tribal people in Wayanad, Kerala. *Rajagiri Journal of Social Development*, *3*(1&2), 7-36.

39. Johny, O. K. (2001). Wayanad Rekhakal (Malayalam). Pappiyo.

40. Kannamudaiyar, S., & Chellasamy, P. (2023). Impact of Trifed on Livelihood Security of Tribal Households: A Special Reference to Nilgiris District, Tamilnadu. *IJFMR-International Journal For Multidisciplinary Research*, *5*(2).

41. Kerala forest Administrative report (2021). Kerala Forest and Wildlife Department, Government of Kerala.

42. Kerala Forest Department (2018).Working Plan Vazhachal Division, Government of Kerala.

43. Kerala Forest Department (2021).Working Plan Marayoor Division, Government of Kerala.

44. Kerala Forest Statistics Report (2020). Kerala forest statistics report. Kerala Forest and Wildlife Department, Government of Kerala.

45. Kerala Institute for Research Training & Development Studies of Scheduled Castes and Scheduled Tribes (KIRTADS). (n.d). Tribals in Kerala. Retrieved January 8, 2023, from https://kirtads.kerala.gov.in/tribals-in-kerala/

46. Kjosavik, D. J., & Shanmugaratnam, N. (2021). The persistent Adivasi demand for land rights and the Forest Rights Act 2006 in Kerala, India. *Social Sciences*, *10*(5), 158.

47. Krishnan, S., & Mallick, S. (2023). The Forest Rights Act and Adivasi Landlessness in Kerala. *Journal of Asian and African Studies*, 00219096231153148.

48. Kurup, A. M. (1971). Status of Kerala scheduled tribes: A study based on ethno-demographic data. *Economic and Political Weekly*, 1815-1820.

49. L.P. George, & Alexander, G. (2023). Role of Participatory Forest Management Institutions in the Management of Non-Timber Forest Products: A Road Map from Kerala. *Indian Forester,* 149 (9).

50. L.P.George. (2021) Vanaparipalathine Kootaymadu Karuthu (Malayalam). Forestry Information Bureau. Government of Kerala. *Aranyam Magazine* 41(11-12).

51. L.P.George.(2023) Kaal Nootandu Pinnidunna Pankalitha Vana Paripalanam (Malayalam). Forestry Information Bureau. Government of Kerala. *Aranyam Magazine* 43(7).

52. Masuda, M., Mishiba, J., & Dhakal, M. (2005). Implementation of participatory forest management in Kerala, India. Tropics, 14(4), 323-333.

53. Mathavan, S., & Miller, P. L. (1989). A collection of dragonflies (Odonata) made in the Periyar National Park, Kerala, South India, in January, 1988. *Rapid communications, 10*(1), 1-10.

54. Mendes, Luke. (2021). Grasses and Grassland Ecosystems. Paper for Intechopen Limited.

55. MOEF (Ministry of Environment and Forests), Government of India. (2009). Report to the people on environment and forests: 2009–2010.

56. Mohanty, A. (2015). A study on the implementation status of the Forest Right Act, 2006 at the national and state levels and its recommendations. *Journal of North East India Studies, 5*(1), 73-91.

57. Mohindra, K. S., Narayana, D., Harikrishnadas, C. K., Anushreedha, S. S., & Haddad, S. (2010). Paniya voices: a participatory poverty and health assessment among a marginalized South Indian tribal population. *BMC Public Health, 10*, 1-9.

58. Münster, U., & Vishnudas, S. (2012). In the jungle of law: Adivasi rights and implementation of forest rights act in Kerala. *Economic and Political Weekly*, 38-45.

59. Muraleedharan, P. K., Sasidharan, N., Kumar, B. M., Sreenivasan, M. A., & Seethalakshmi, K. K. (2005). Non-timber forest products in the Western Ghats of India: floristic attributes extraction and regeneration. *Journal of Tropical Forest Science*, 17(2): 243-257.

60. Narayanan, M. R., Anilkumar, N., Balakrishnan, V., Sivadasan, M., Alfarhan, H. A., & Alatar, A. A. (2011). Wild edible plants used by the Kattunaikka, Paniya, and Kuruma tribes of Wayanad District, Kerala, India. *J Med Plants Res*, 5(15), 3520-3529.

61. Newton, N. M. (2019). Impact of participatory forest management on the livelihoods of indigenous communities (Doctoral dissertation, Department of Natural Resource Management College of Forestry, Vellanikkara).

62. Padmanabhan, P. (2007). *Ethno zoological studies on the tribals of Palakkad and Malappuram districts of Kerala, South India* (No. 292). KFRI Research Report.

63. Panda, R. 1998. Tribal Problems: A Study from Micro in S.N.Tripathy (Ed.) Tribals in India – the Changing Scenario. New Delhi: Discovery Publishing House.

64. Pandey, A. K., Tripathi, Y. C., & Kumar, A. (2016). Non-timber forest products (NTFPs) for sustained livelihood: Challenges and strategies. *Research Journal of Forestry*, 10(1), 1-7.

65. Parameswaran, M. P. (1979). Significance of Silent Valley. *Economic and Political Weekly*, 1117-1119.

66. Perera, J. (2009). Scheduled Tribes and Other Traditional Forest Dwellers (Recognition of Forest Rights) Act 2006: A Charter of Forest Dwellers' Rights?. *Land and Cultural Survival*, 213.

67. Pillai, R. (2010). Eco-development and Tribal Empowerment. MPRA Paper No. 22202 DOI- https://mpra.ub.uni-muenchen.de/22202/

68. Radhakrishnan, K., Pandurangan, A.G., 2000. The role of tribal medicine in local health care with reference to Kerala. In: Proceedings of the Twelfth Kerala Science Congress, Kumily, Kerala, pp. 864–866.

69. Ramachandran, B. (1997). Ethnographic notes on the Kattunaickens a food-gathering tribe of Wayanad, Kerala. *Journal of Human Ecology*, *8*(4), 293-295.

70. Rammohan, K. T., Soman, S., & Joseph, E. (2015). Munnar: Through the lens of political ecology. *Economic and Political Weekly*, 33-37.

71. Ranganatha, B. (2014). Tribal Identity and the Implications for Political and Cultural Development: A Sociological Analysis. *International Journal of Applied Science and Engineering*, *2*(1), 27-40.

72. Ranjith, M. (2021). Responsible tourism as best practices for sustainable ecotourism-a case of kumarakom in Kerala. International Journal of Tourism & Hotel Business Management (IJTHBM), 3(3), 485-498.

73. Sadath, A., Kabir, Z., KM, J., & Uthaman, S. P. (2023). Smoking, betel quid chewing, and alcohol use among an indigenous primitive Tribal group in the Kerala State of India: Secondary analysis of a Tribal household survey. *Journal of Ethnicity in Substance Abuse*, 1-16.

74. Sandhya, S., Vinod, K. R., Sekhar, J. C., Aradhana, R., & Nath, V. S. (2010). An updated review on *Tricosanthes cucumerina* L. *Int. J. Pharm. Sci. Rev. Res*, *1*(2), 56-58.

75. Sasidharan,N.(1998). Studies On The Flora Of Periyar Tiger Reserve, KFRI Research Report 150.

76. Satish.A, (2017, 27 August). 'Wheels of change transform the lives of Attappadi women'. The New Indian Express: Kerala Edition.

77. Saxena, N. C. (1997). The saga of participatory forest management in India. CIFOR.

78. Schreckenberg, K., & Luttrell, C. (2009). Participatory forest management: a route to poverty reduction? *International Forestry Review*, *11*(2), 221-238.

79. Shackleton, C. M., & de Vos, A. (2022). How many people globally actually use non-timber forest products?. *Forest Policy and Economics*, *135*, 102659.

80. Shahapurmath, G., & Hanumatha, M. (2015). Present Status And Distribution Pattern Of Sandalwood With Its Culture And Heritage Values Across The Globe. *Journal of Plant Development Sciences*, *7*(5), 401-407.

81. Sharma, R. A. (1995). Participatory forest management in India. Ambio, 131-133.

82. Shihab, H. (2020). Issues of alcoholism dependence among tribes: how Koraga tribal population of Kerala find their everyday life. *International Journal of Indian Psychology*, *8*(1).

83. Shiva, M. P. (1995). Collection, utilization, and marketing of Medicinal plants from the forests of India. *RAP Publication (FAO)*.

84. Shylajan, C. S., & Mythili, G. (2007). Community dependence on non-timber forest products: A household analysis and its implication for forest conservation. Indra Gandhi Institute of Development Research, Research Report No. WP, 5, 29.

85. Singh, J. S., Singh, S. P., Saxena, A. K., & Rawat, Y. S. (1984). India's Silent Valley and its threatened rain-forest ecosystems. *Environmental conservation*, *11*(3), 223-233.

86. Soman, D., & Anitha, V. (2020). Community dependence on the natural resources of Parambikulam Tiger Reserve, Kerala, India. *Trees, Forests and People*, *2*, 100014.

87. Squires, V. R., Dengler, J., Hua, L., & Feng, H. (Eds.). (2018). *Grasslands of the world: diversity, management and conservation*. CRC Press.

88. Sreenivasan, M. A., Sasidharan, N., Seethalakshmi, K. K., Muraleedharan, P. K., & Kumar, B. M. (2005). Non-timber forest products in the Western Ghats of India: floristic attributes extraction and regeneration.

89. Suganthi, N., Sujeetha, T. N., Anamica, M., & Venkata, P. (2017). Perceived Economic Empowerment of the Tribal Community. *Biosciences*, 8057.

90. T G Nair, Vinodkumar & Kunju, Navas & Mathew, Angala & Chandrapal, Ajitha. (2016). Traditional Food Habits Of Tribal Communities of Idukki District in Kerala.

91. Talukdar, N. R., Choudhury, P., Barbhuiya, R. A., & Singh, B. (2021). Importance of non-timber forest products (NTFPs) in rural livelihood: A study in Patharia Hills Reserve Forest, northeast India. *Trees, Forests and People*, *3*, 100042.

92. Thampi, S. P. (2005). Ecotourism in Kerala, India: Lessons from the eco-development project in Periyar Tiger Reserve (Vol. 13). ECOCLUB, E-Paper Series, Nr. 13, June 2005.

93. Thimm, T., & Karlaganis, C. (2020). A conceptual framework for indigenous ecotourism projects–a case study in Wayanad, Kerala, India. *Journal of Heritage Tourism*, *15*(3), 294-311.

94. Thimm, T., & Karlaganis, C. (2020). A conceptual framework for indigenous ecotourism projects–a case study in Wayanad, Kerala, India. *Journal of Heritage Tourism*, *15*(3), 294-311.

95. Thimm, T., & Karlaganis, C. (2020). A conceptual framework for indigenous ecotourism projects–a case study in Wayanad, Kerala, India. Journal of Heritage Tourism, 15(3), 294-311.

96. Turner, R. L. (2004). Communities, wildlife conservation, and tourism-based development: Can community-based nature tourism live up to its promise?. *Journal of International Wildlife Law and Policy*, 7(3-4), 161-182.

97. Ullas,A.S,(2021,2 December).Kerala No 1 in alcohol consumption, Alappuzha leads among districts'.Malayala Manorama Online.Retrieved from https://www.onmanorama.com/news/kerala/2021/12/02/alcohol-consumption-highest-in-kerala-indian-states-alappuzha-malappuram.html

98. V. S. Sreeraj, S. P. (2012). Reasons for Substance Use: A Comparative Study of Alcohol Use in Tribals and Non-tribals. Indian Journal of Psychological Medicine, 242-46.

99. Vinodan, A. (2010). Assessing Institutional Competencies Of Ecotourism; Special Reference To Thenmala Ecotourism Project Kerala, India. *ASEAN Journal on Hospitality and Tourism*, 9(2), 101-118.

100. Vinodan, A., & Manalel, J. A. M. E. S. (2011). Local economic benefits of ecotourism: A case study on Parambikulan Tiger Reserve in Kerala, India. South Asian journal of tourism and heritage, 4(2), 93-109.

101. Weaver, D. B., & Lawton, L. J. (2007). Twenty years on: The state of contemporary ecotourism research. *Tourism Management, 28*(5), 1168-1179.

102. World Health Organization. (2019). *Global status report on alcohol and health 2018.* World Health Organization.

103. Yesodharan, K., and K. A. Sujana. "Wild edible plants traditionally used by the tribes in the Parambikulam Wildlife Sanctuary, Kerala, India." (2007). Natural Product Radiance, Vol. 6(1), 2007, pp.74-80.

Abbreviations

ACF	Assistant Conservator of Forests
APCCF	Additional Principal Chief Conservator of Forests
AVSS	Adivasi Vana Samraksha Samithi
BFO	Beet Forest Officer
CF	Conservator of Forests
DCF	Deputy Conservator of Forests
E&TW	Eco-development & Tribal Welfare
EDC	Eco-development Committee
EDO	Eco-development Officer
FDA	Forest Development Agency
FCAA	Forest (Conservation) Amendment Act
FRA	Forest Rights Act
GO	Government Order
GST	Goods and Services Tax
IFS	Indian Forest Service
IIST	Indian Institute of Space Science and Technology
ISRO	Indian Space Research Organization
KFD	Kerala Forest Department
MFP	Minor Forest Produce
MSP for MFP	Minimum Support Price for Minor Forest Produce
MVD	Motor Vehicle Department
NAP	National Afforestation Program
NGO	Non-governmental Organization
NTFP	Non-timber Forest Product

PCCF	Principal Chief Conservator of Forests
PFM	Participatory Forest Management
PRA	Participatory Rural Appraisal
PTR	Periyar Tiger Reserve
PVTG	Particularly Vulnerable Tribal Group
RFO	Range Forest Officer
SFDA	State Forest Development Agency
SFO	Section Forest Officer
SHG	Self-help Group
SUPPLYCO	Kerala State Civil Supplies Corporation Limited
TRIFED	Tribal Co-operative Marketing Development Federation
VSS	Vana Samraksha Samithi
WLPO	Wildlife Preservation Officer

Acronyms

VSS/EDC (PFM Institutions)

Vana Samraksha Samithi and the Eco-development Committee are fundamental PFM institutions at the grassroots level that empower forest-dependent communities to actively participate in forest conservation and sustainable development initiatives. Vana Samraksha Samithis are typically established in fringe areas adjacent to forest lands, while Eco-development Committees are primarily formed within protected wildlife areas. Both institutions serve as platforms for implementing collaborative projects and programs that align with the principles of participatory forest management.

State Forest Development Agency (SFDA)

The State Forest Development Agency (SFDA), an autonomous body constituted in 2010, is the apex body of 36 Forest Development Agencies (FDAs) in the state. It is also the nodal agency for various projects and oversees the execution of PFM programs. The State Forest Development Agency (SFDA) serves as a "special purpose vehicle" dedicated to advancing Participatory Forest Management (PFM) initiatives.

Forest Development Agency (FDA)

An FDA is a confederation of PFM institutions (Vana Samrakshana Samithi - VSS) and Eco-Development Committee - EDC) affiliated with the SFDA, through which PFM activities are implemented at the grassroots level. They are autonomous bodies constituted in line with the Forest Divisions for the execution of PFM Programs.

Microplan

A microplan is a localized document created in collaboration with forest-dependent communities to guide the overall management of PFM institutions. This plan strives to promote the active participation of villagers in the responsible utilization of resources. Additionally, it seeks to evaluate the level of reliance of communities on forest resources.

PVTGs

Particularly Vulnerable Tribal Groups (PVTGs) are a group of tribal communities in India that are recognized as being the most vulnerable among the Scheduled Tribes. There are 75 PVTGs identified in India, and they are spread across 18 states and Union Territories. PVTGs are characterized by their small populations, isolated geographical locations, lack of access to basic amenities, and low literacy rates. They are also often marginalized and discriminated against due to their cultural and linguistic differences.

Lucky Bill App

The Lucky Bill App is an innovative platform introduced by the Kerala Government to encourage consumers to request bills for their purchases. This platform allows consumers in Kerala to upload bills, participate in lucky draws, and win exciting prizes.

Haritha Karma Sena

The Haritha Karma Sena (HKS) is a waste management initiative in Kerala, India, that aims to provide employment and income by collecting and treating waste. It is a micro-entrepreneurial initiative under the Kudumbashree Mission, a state-level poverty eradication and women empowerment program.

Indian Institute of Space Science and Technology (IIST)

IIST is a government-aided institute and deemed university for the study and research of space science, located in Thiruvananthapuram, India. IIST was set up in 2007 by the Indian Space Research Organization (ISRO) under the Department of Space, Government of India. The institute offers undergraduate, postgraduate, and doctoral programs in space science, technology, and applications. IIST also conducts research in a wide range of space-related fields, including astronomy, astrophysics, atmospheric physics, planetary science, space engineering, and satellite technology.

NTFPs

Non-timber forest products (NTFPs) are any product or service produced in forests other than timber. They play a vital role in the livelihoods of forest-dependent communities, providing them with food, medicine, income, and other essential resources. NTFPs encompass a wide range of products, including various types of honey, turmeric, tree bark, nuts, dammar, clove, cardamom, wild ginger, pepper, etc.

Ecotourism

Ecotourism is a form of tourism that involves visiting natural areas while respecting the environment and supporting the local communities. It is a form of responsible travel that focuses on minimizing negative impacts and maximizing positive ones. Ecotourism activities can include hiking, camping, wildlife viewing, birdwatching, etc.

Medicinal Plants

Medicinal plants are a diverse group of plants that have been used for centuries to treat a variety of ailments. They are an important source of natural medicine and continue to be used in many parts of the world today. Arogyapacha, Brahmi, Chukkul, Ashwagandha, and Kattupadavalam are examples of medicinal plants found in Kerala.

Eco-restoration

Ecological restoration is the process of assisting the recovery of an ecosystem that has been degraded, damaged, or destroyed. It aims to restore the ecosystem to its original state or to a state that is closely related to its original state.

Invasive Plants (Exotic Species)

Invasive plants are non-native plants that have been introduced to a new environment where they are able to spread and reproduce without natural limits, causing harm to the native ecosystem and human activities. These plants can pose a significant threat to biodiversity, economic stability, and human health.

www.ingramcontent.com/pod-product-compliance
Lightning Source LLC
Chambersburg PA
CBHW020320290526
45785CB00007B/2860